The Alchemist

IN LIFE, LITERATURE, AND ART

John Read

*Professor of Chemistry in the University of St. Andrews formerly
Professor of Organic Chemistry in the University of Sydney, Australia*

ISBN 1-56459-210-3

Request our FREE CATALOG of over 1,000
Rare Esoteric Books
Unavailable Elsewhere

Alchemy, Ancient Wisdom, Astronomy, Baconian, Eastern-Thought, Egyptology, Esoteric, Freemasonry, Gnosticism, Hermetic, Magic, Metaphysics, Mysticism, Mystery Schools, Mythology, Occult, Philosophy, Psychology, Pyramids, Qabalah, Religions, Rosicrucian, Science, Spiritual, Symbolism, Tarot, Theosophy, *and many more!*

Kessinger Publishing Company
Montana, U.S.A.

THE 'LABORATORY
(Teniers)

PREFACE

I N two foregoing books, *Prelude to Chemistry* and *Humour and Humanism in Chemistry*, the author has tried to sketch in simple terms, appealing alike to the general reader and the specialist, some of the outstanding humanistic and cultural elements of alchemy and of alchemy's daughter, chemistry.

As is now shown more concisely in the early part of the present book, mythology and religion, astrology and magic, mysticism and science, literature and art, and many another ingredient—including even music—have contributed to the rise and development of alchemy, and hence of chemistry, the most romantic and picturesque of all the manifold fields of science.

Focused against this variegated background, stands out in bold relief that strange and fantastic being, the alchemist. It is with the alchemist, who has suffered so much neglect since alchemy was outmoded by modern chemistry in the second half of the eighteenth century, that the following pages are chiefly concerned. In them, the alchemist is first considered realistically in relation to his working background of alchemy, with its intriguing theories and conceptions, its vast literature, and its wealth of cryptic expression and pictorial symbolism. The survey then passes from the living model to a contemplation of various idealistic presentations of the alchemist, in literature, and also in pictorial art.

In *Prelude to Chemistry* literature and pictorial art were considered as ingredients of alchemy. The complementary view is now afforded of the alchemist as a vivid figure in literature and pictorial art, especially as seen in the varied impressions to be found in the writings of Chaucer and Ben Jonson and in the genre paintings of the Flemish and Dutch

PREFACE

artists. This subject, so full of fascination for the discerning man of science as well as for the lover of literature and art, has received surprisingly little attention, possibly because it calls for a blending of interests often wrongly supposed to be as hard to immingle as oil and water.

The present treatment is based largely upon articles that have appeared at various times in *Endeavour*, *The Burlington Magazine*, *Ambix*, *Scientia*, and *Nature*. The author's grateful acknowledgments are made to the editors of these publications, and also to Mr. R. B. Pilcher, O.B.E., for a photograph of the engraving of Simon Forman. Most of the illustrations have been prepared from items in the collection gathered by the author in the Chemistry Department of the United College of St. Salvator and St. Leonard, in the University of St. Andrews.

J. R.

THE UNIVERSITY
ST. ANDREWS, SCOTLAND

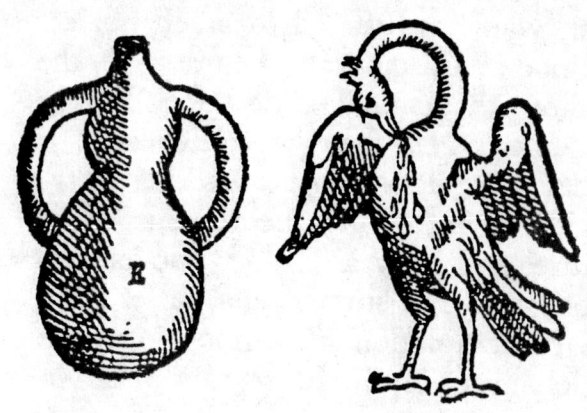

CONTENTS

	Page
PREFACE	v
TITLES AND DESCRIPTIONS OF THE ILLUSTRATIONS	viii

CHAPTER I

ALCHEMY AND ALCHEMISTS	1
Nature and Origin of Alchemy	1
Alchemical Theory	3
Some Alchemical Tenets	9
Operations of the Great Work	13
Alchemical Expression and Symbolism	16
Types of Alchemists	23

CHAPTER II

THE ALCHEMIST IN LITERATURE	25
Introductory	25
An Alchemist among the Canterbury Pilgrims	29
An Alchemist in Jacobean London	39
An Alchemist tells of Himself	47

CHAPTER III

THE ALCHEMIST IN ART	56
Introductory	56
Dürer's "Melencolia"	57
Weiditz	62
Brueghel	63
Stradanus	66
de Bry	68
The Mystical Alchemist in Art	68
Teniers	72
van Ostade	79
Steen	80
Bega	81
Wijck	81
Other Dutch Painters	84
A Spanish Alchemical Painting	85
Later Alchemical Paintings	86
Wright of Derby	88
REFERENCES	91
GLOSSARY	92
INDEX	95

LIST OF PLATES

THE 'LABORATORY . . . . . *Colour Frontispiece*
From a painting (1793) by J. J. Rink after D. Teniers. This faithful copy, in the St. Andrews collection, measures 16 by 12·5 inches

at page

1. A Representation of the Sulphur-Mercury Theory of Metals 8
From *Viridarium Chymicum*, D. Stolcius, Frankfurt, 1624 (reprinted therein from *Symbola Aureae Mensae Duodecim Nationum*, M. Maier, Frankfurt, 1617)

2. The Stone of Saturn 9
From *Atalanta Fugiens*, M. Maier, Oppenheim, 1618

3. The Vase of Hermes in the Athanor 16
From *Elementa Chemiae*, J. C. Barchusen, Leyden, 1718

4. The First Key of Basil Valentine 17
From *Viridarium Chymicum*, D. Stolcius, Frankfurt, 1624 (reprinted therein from *Tripus Aureus*, M. Maier, Frankfurt, 1618)

5. An Emblematic Representation of the Great Work . 24
From *Viridarium Chymicum*, D. Stolcius, Frankfurt, 1624

6. "Aim at this carefully with the fiery sword" . . 25
From *Secretioris Naturae Secretorum Scrutinium Chymicum*, M. Maier, Frankfurt, 1687 (reprinted therein from *Atalanta Fugiens*, M. Maier, Oppenheim, 1618)

7. Geoffrey Chaucer (c. 1340–1400) 32
From a reproduction of Occleve's portrait in *The Gallery of Portraits: with Memoirs*, Vol. III, Charles Knight, London, 1834

8. An Alchemist and his Assistant at Work . . . 33
From a woodcut by Hans Weiditz (c. 1520)

9. Ben Jonson (1573–1617) 40
Gerard Honthorst pinxit, Philip Audinet sculp.

10. Title-page of the first edition of *The Alchemist* . 44-45
Published in quarto, London, 1612. The rule measures 9·4 cm. in the original. By courtesy of the Trustees of the British Museum

11. A page from the first edition of *The Alchemist*, London, 1612 44-45
(Act II: Subtle, Mammon, Surly.) The bottom line of the text is 7·0 cm. wide in the original. By courtesy of the Trustees of the British Museum

LIST OF PLATES

at page

12 David Garrick as Abel Drugger in *The Alchemist* . . 48
From a mezzotint after J. Zoffany (c. 1770), measuring 22·5 by 18 inches. "This fellow, captain, will come, in time, to be a great distiller"

13 Simon Forman (1552–1611) 49
A print "engraved from the Original Drawing in the Collection of the Right Honble. Lord Mountstuart, Bulfinch del. Godfrey sc.," published by F. Blyth, No. 87 Cornhill, London, in 1776. A reversed print was published by James Caulfield, in 1793

14 Melencolia 56
From the copper-plate engraving by Albrecht Dürer (1514). Facsimile-Reproduction der Reichsdruckerei, Berlin

15 An Alchemist at Work 57
After Pieter Brueghel (1558), from the plate engraved by H. Cock and retouched by T. Galle, measuring 44·5 by 33·5 cm.

16 Pvlvis Pyrivs 64
Ioan. Stradanus iuent. Phls. Galle excud. (c. 1570). The original is 26·5 cm. wide

17 The Oratory and the Laboratory 65
H. F. Vriese pinxit. Paullus van der Doort, Antwerp, sculpsit. From *Amphitheatrum Sapientiae Æternae*, H. Khunrath, Hanau, 1609

18 David Teniers (1610–94) 68
This representation of an alchemist by Teniers is supposed to be a self-portrait

19 Le Chimiste 69
Peint par David Teniers. Gravé à l'eau-forte par Michon. Et terminé par Lorieux. The original is 20·7 cm. wide

20 An Alchemist in his Laboratory 72
From the Hanfstaengl print of an engraving by C. Straub after D. Teniers, 50·0 cm. wide

21 An Alchemical Interior 73
Sometimes known as "Le Grimoire d'Hypocrate." From the original painting by D. Teniers

22 Alchemical Cupids 76
From the original painting by D. Teniers

23 The Alchemist 76-77
From the original painting by Jan Steen

24 L'Alchymiste en Méditation 76-77
Peint par Th. With. Dessiné par Gianni. Gravé par V. Texier. The original is 25·8 cm. wide

25 Le Ménage du Chimiste 77
Thomas Wyck pinx. P. Chenu sculp. A Paris chés Basan graveur. The original is 49·8 cm. wide

LIST OF PLATES

                                                                                            at page

26 A Spanish Alchemical Painting   80
      Painter unknown. In the St. Andrews collection. The original measures about 38 by 28 inches

27 Chemistry   81
      R. Corbould del. J. Chapman sc. London. Published as the Act directs. July 27, 1805, by J. Wilkes. The original is 17·7 cm. wide

28 Hocus Pocus or Searching for the Philosophers Stone   84
      T. Rowlandson, 1800. Pub. March 12, 1800, at R. Ackermans Repository of Arts, N 101, Strand. The original is 32·0 cm. wide

29 The Discovery of Phosphorus   85
      Josh. Wright pinxt. Wm. Pether fecit. Published Sepr. 1^t, 1775, & sold by W. Pether in Broad St^t, St. James's. The original measures about 22 by 18 inches

ILLUSTRATIONS IN THE TEXT

The ornamental Initial Letters and Finis are reproduced from *De Distillatione, Lib. IX*, J. B. Porta, Romae, 1608

The Alchemical Pelican   vi
      From *De Distillatione, Lib. IX*, J. B. Porta, Romae, 1608

The Four Qualities and Four Elements   3

The Alchemical Bear   24
      From *Ars Destillatoria*, J. B. Porta, Frankfurt, 1611

The Alchemical Stork   55
      From *Ars Destillatoria*, J. B. Porta, Frankfurt, 1611

Ennobling the Base Metals   90
      From *Viridarium Chymicum*, D. Stolcius, Frankfurt, 1624

The Alchemical Ostrich   94
      From *Ars Destillatoria*, J. B. Porta, Frankfurt, 1611

TO THE MEMORY OF
THE ARTIST OF ALCHEMY *PAR EXCELLENCE*
**DAVID TENIERS
THE
YOUNGER**

                              The philosophre stoon,
Elixir clept, we seeken it each one,
For had we him, then were we sure y-nough;
But unto God of heven I make avow,
For al oure craft, when we have al y-do,
And al oure sleight, he wol not come us to.
He hath i-made us spende moche good,
For sorrow of which almost we waxen wood,
But that good hope crepeth in oure herte,
Supposing ever, though we sore smerte,
To be relievèd by him after-ward.
Such súpposing and hope is sharp and hard.
I warne you wel it is to seken ever.
That future time hath made men dissevere,
In trust thereof, from al that ever they hadde.
Yet of that art thay never wexe sadde,
For unto them it is a bitter swete;
So semeth it; for had thay but a sheete
In which thay mighte wrappe them for the night,
And eek a cloke to walke inne by day-light,
They wolde them selle, and spenden on this craft;
Thay can nought stinte, til no thing be laft.
                                        CHAUCER

Nature and Origin of Alchemy

ALCHEMY, often narrowly defined as the pretended art of transmuting base metals into silver and gold, was in reality a grandiose system of philosophy, embodying a field of human beliefs and ideas vast in range and extending in time over a period of more than a thousand years. In the mid-nineteenth century, when scientific chemistry was still young, Liebig pointed out the injustice of confounding alchemy with gold-making. "Alchemy was a science," he wrote, "and included all those processes in which chemistry was technically applied. Among the alchemists there was always to be found a nucleus of genuine philosophers, who often deceived themselves in their theoretical views; whereas the gold-makers properly so-called, knowingly deceived both themselves and others."[1]

Even Liebig, however, took a restricted view of alchemy; for the complex ramifications of this great corpus of human imagination and experience drew ideas richly from philosophy and religion and spread out into astrology, occultism, magic, mythology, and other strange fields. From the point of view of the true adepts, the spectacular attempts to raise the base metals to the perfection of gold, by transmutation, were merely of interest in so far as they might afford material evidence of the truth of a philosophical system which was concerned alike with the formation of inanimate substances and the still more formidable mysteries of life. The arbitrary and uninformed operations of mercenary gold-makers were nothing more than a debasement of the real alchemy.

[1] Ref. 9, p. 91

This broad view of alchemy, in particular its intimate relationships with religion, philosophy, and psychology, have too often been overlooked by writers and commentators; in psychology, for example, the discernment of a master was necessary in order to bring out the fundamental truth that alchemy is no less important in this field of knowledge than in chemistry.[1]

It has been said that the proper study of mankind is man; the study of man calls in turn for an examination of his beliefs and ideas, even when these have been modified or even largely discarded, as in alchemy. Sympathetic studies of alchemy and of its devoted followers, the alchemists, may well be able to point a moral for this modern age, which so often overlooks or despises its origins: this age in which science has outstripped man's abilities to cope with the conditions he has created; in which thought is increasingly dominated by science to the exclusion of faith; and in which higher thought on a moral or spiritual plane is called for, in order to bring about a more rational plan of living and a greater reverence for life and its underlying mysteries.

No definite origin can be ascribed to alchemy. The alchemists often called themselves the "sons of Hermes" and ascribed the origin of their so-called "Hermetic Art" to Hermes the Thrice-Great, a Greek equivalent of the Egyptian god, Thoth. Probably the curious blend of beliefs and ideas upon which alchemy was based came mainly from primitive forms of religion, magic, and general modes of thought. The usual imagined home of alchemy is Egypt, or *Khem*, the Hebrew "Land of Ham"; and it is said that the art was transmitted to Islam under the name of *al Khem*, and thence to the Western world as *alchemy*. Alchemical ideas appear also to have arisen in China so long ago as the fifth century B.C., in close association with the philosophic and religious system of Taoism. Oriental and Occidental ideas of alchemy are so closely parallel as to suggest a common origin. These early alchemical beliefs and practices were eventually influenced during the Alexandrian era (fourth

[1] C. G. Jung, ref. 8

century B.C. to seventh century A.D.) by the views of the Greek philosophers, and the accretive system passed by way of the Islamic writings and their Latin translations into medieval Christendom.

ALCHEMICAL THEORY

Alchemical reasoning and experimental procedure were based upon a complex farrago of ideas, beliefs, and theories. It is usually assumed that the fundamental physical theory of alchemy was that of the Four Elements. Although ascribed as a rule to Aristotle (*c.* 350 B.C.), in its essentials this was recognized both in India and Egypt so early as 1500 B.C., and the Chinese system of the Five Elements is equally old. Going farther back still, the theory of the Four Elements was probably conceived as a development of a primitive mode of thinking depending upon a distinction between pairs of opposites. Aristotle's theory postulated the existence of four fundamental properties or qualities of all material bodies: the hot and the moist, with their contraries the cold and the dry. These abstract entities gave rise by conjugation in pairs to the four elements, earth, air, fire, and water, of which all matter was held to be composed in different proportions. The postulated relationships may be summarized diagrammatically in the following way:

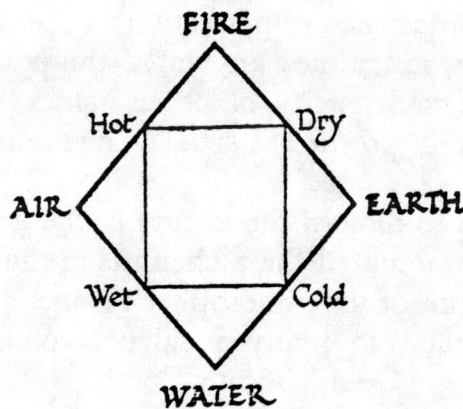

THE FOUR QUALITIES AND FOUR ELEMENTS

Transmutation was an obvious consequence of this theory. For example, when the coldness of water was replaced by heat the cold-wet water changed into hot-wet air, *i.e.* the air-like or gaseous steam. Another outcome of the theory was the idea of a *prima materia*, or primordial matter, from which all bodies were formed and into which they might again be resolved. A further development, arising perhaps in the early centuries of the Christian era, was the conception of a transmuting agent, capable of promoting the change of one kind of material into another : this imagined agent became known as the Philosopher's Stone.

So were evolved the two *a priori* postulates upon which the deductive reasoning of alchemy was mainly based. These were (1) the unity of matter, and (2) the existence of a potent transmuting agent, the philosopher's stone. From the idea of the unity of matter flowed the further assumption that this stone, the medicine of the base metals, would act also as the medicine of man; hence, in the form of the Elixir Vitae or Red Tincture, the stone was depicted as an agent for curing all human ills and conferring longevity. Herein may perhaps be perceived a Greek influence, emanating from the Platonic conception that nothing exists that is not good and from Aristotle's dictum that nature strives always towards perfection. In the mineral kingdom, according to the tenets of alchemy, ordinary perfection was attained in gold, and the quintessence of perfection in the philosopher's stone. The stone, sometimes known as the powder of projection and by a multiplicity of other names, was usually visualized as a red powder, fixed, heavy, and having a pleasant odour.

We now begin to discern the nature of the extraordinary motive power that actuated the alchemists in the elusive and never-ending pursuit of the philosopher's stone, in the course of which they made so many incidental observations of chemical interest. "Gold," wrote Goethe, "gives power; without health there is no enjoyment, and longevity here takes the place of immortality." In this simple sentence lies the mainspring of a stupendous driving force that remained active throughout some forty generations of alchemists, for more than a millennium. The quest of the philosopher's stone is the greatest odyssey in the history of science. So great may be the power of an idea.

Without the thought of the philosopher's stone acting powerfully and constantly on the minds and faculties of men, as Liebig pointed out, "chemistry would not now stand in its present position. . . . In order to know that the philosopher's stone did not really exist, it was indispensable that every substance accessible to study and observation should be observed and examined, in accordance with the scientific resources of the time. But it is precisely in this that we perceive the almost miraculous influence of the idea. The strength of opinion could not be broken, till science had reached a certain stage of development. . . . We hear it said that the idea of the philosopher's stone was an error, but all our views have been developed from errors, and that which to-day we regard as truth in chemistry may, perhaps, before to-morrow, be recognized as a fallacy."

Of more immediate interest to medieval alchemy than the theory of the Four Elements was the sulphur-mercury theory of the composition of metals, first encountered in the Islamic writings and Latinized versions ascribed to Jabir, or Geber, a somewhat elusive figure of the ninth century. In its bare essentials, the sulphur-mercury theory was a simplified and more concrete expression of the Aristotelian pair of opposites denoted by the terms "fire" and "water." The interpretation of alchemical terms was always elastic. Thus "fire" might signify energy or the principle of combustibility, and "water" became the embodiment of liquidity; similarly, "earth" and "air" might typify what are now known as the solid and gaseous states of aggregation of matter, respectively. In the words of Muir, "all liquid substances were supposed to be liquid because they possessed something in common; this hypothetical something was called the *Element, Water*. Similarly, the view prevailed until comparatively recent times, that burning substances burn because of the presence in them of a hypothetical, imponderable fluid, called ' *Caloric* '; the alchemists preferred to call this indefinable something an Element, and to name it *Fire*."

Fire and water were by far the more important of the two pairs of Aristotelian elements, and they descended into the sulphur-mercury theory of metals with little essential alteration except in name. " Fire " became " sulphur " and " water " became " mercury." " Sulphur " represented combustibility, and " mercury " represented fusibility, metallicity, or the mineral spirit of metals. The " sulphur " and " mercury " of the philosophers, known often as " sophic sulphur " and " sophic mercury," or " our sulphur " and " our mercury," were not identified with the ordinary material substances having these names, although they were denoted by the same symbols; they were rather abstractions, standing for combinations of properties or qualities, which to some extent were reminiscent of those of the two material substances.

To quote an unknown medieval writer, who used the name of Roger Bacon to lend authority to his pronouncements, according to a common alchemical practice: " The natural principles in the mynes, are *Argent-vive* [Mercury], and *Sulphur*. All mettalls and minerals, whereof there be sundrie and divers kinds, are begotten of these two: but I must tel you, that nature alwaies intendeth and striveth to the perfection of Gold: but many accidents coming between, change the mettalls. . . . For according to the puritie and impuritie of the two aforesaid principles, *Argent-vive*, and *Sulphur*, pure and impure mettalls are ingendred."

According to this theory, impure sulphur and mercury when conjoined led to the formation of base metals such as quicksilver, tin, and lead; sulphur and mercury of ordinary purity produced gold; and quintessentialized sulphur and mercury gave rise to a superfine form of gold known as the philosopher's stone. The stone was held to exceed ordinary gold so infinitely in purity as to be able to transmute or " tinge " a very large amount of a base metal into ordinary gold.

"*Mare tingerem, si mercurius esset!*—I would tinge the sea [into gold], if it were quicksilver!" exclaimed another unknown writer using the name of Raymond Lully and adopting the grandiloquent air so often to be found in alchemical treatises.

The sulphur-mercury theory is represented vividly in an engraving of 1617 (Plate 1). The two kinds of natural exhalations "in the mynes," marked with the alchemical symbols for sulphur (left) and mercury (right), are shown in the process of conjunction, or reaction, in the bowels of the earth, whereby "pure and impure mettalls are ingendred." Above, on the crust of the earth, an alchemist is engaged in the operations of the Great Work of preparing the philosopher's stone through the operations of art, here contrasted with those of nature.

Sophic sulphur and sophic mercury were often depicted as masculine and feminine principles, which by their conjunction led to the birth of the philosopher's stone, sometimes represented as an infant. Such beliefs led to the alchemical identification of sophic sulphur and sophic mercury as the counterparts of man's spirit and soul, and to the eventual introduction of "salt" (or "magnesia") as the counterpart of his body. So arose the system of the *tria prima*, or three "hypostatical principles," developed particularly by Paracelsus (1493-1541), the father of a new alchemical era known as the era of iatrochemistry, or chemistry in the service of medicine. Salt, the third principle of the alchemical triangle (as the system was often represented symbolically), stood in a material sense for the principle of uninflammability and fixidity, and in a mystical sense for the body of man.

"Know, then," wrote Paracelsus, "that all the seven metals are born from a threefold matter.... Mercury is the spirit, Sulphur is the soul, and Salt is the body ... the soul, which indeed is Sulphur ... unites those two contraries, the body and spirit, and changes them into one essence." The main attributes and relationships of the *tria prima* are set out in the following summary:

Mercury	Sulphur	Salt
Metallicity, fusibility	Inflammability	Uninflammability, fixidity
Volatile, and unchanged in the fire	Volatile, and changed in the fire	Found in the ashes
Spirit	Soul	Body
Water	Air	Earth

Sulphur and mercury, the masculine and feminine principles, were often represented as fixed and volatile respectively, although this classification is somewhat at variance with the above scheme; but strict consistency is a missing element in alchemy.

In another place, Paracelsus referred to these three principles as phlegma, fat, and ash. "The phlegma is Mercurius, the fat is Sulphur, and the ash is Salt. For that which smokes and evaporates over the fire [as in the burning of wood] is Mercury; what flames and is burnt is Sulphur; and all ash is Salt."

Paracelsus, in the main a propagandist of the Renaissance, was a pioneer in the liberation of alchemy from the medieval obsession of gold-making. After his day, through the work of such alchemists of the later period as Libavius (1540–1616), van Helmont (1577–1644), and Glauber (1604–68), alchemy gradually shed its accretions of mysticism and obscurantism—which eventually maintained a hold only upon a dwindling body of fervent enthusiasts. Thus it came about that in 1661 Robert Boyle was able to publish *The Sceptical Chymist*, which dismissed the system of the four elements and the three hypostatical principles, and introduced the modern idea of an element.

More than a century elapsed, however, between the publication of *The Sceptical Chymist* and the advent of modern chemistry. During this Indian summer of alchemy the stage was held by the Theory of Phlogiston, whilst the four elements and the three hypostatical principles hovered behind the scenes like ghosts reluctant to be laid. Phlogiston, an imagined inflammable principle present in all combustible bodies, was essentially a revival of sophic sulphur, claim-

Plate 1 A Representation of the Sulphur-Mercury Theory (*page 7*)
(Maier)

Plate 2 The Stone of Saturn (*page 11*)
(Maier)

ing noble descent from the Sun-god of the primitive religions. Phlogiston melted finally " into air, into thin air " with the discovery, in the second half of the eighteenth century, of the chemical composition of the ancient " elements " air and water and of the true nature of combustion. These discoveries ushered in the era of modern chemistry.[1]

Some Alchemical Tenets

Many of the subsidiary tenets of alchemy were derived from religion and astrology, and others came from Greek sources. Through astrology, sophic sulphur and gold were linked with the sun (Sol) and sophic mercury and silver with the moon (Luna), whence the associations were carried back to the Sun-god and Moon-goddess of early religious systems. Through astrology also arose the Chaldean practice of associating the seven metals with the seven prominent heavenly bodies and with human organs and destinies. As Chaucer expressed it in the fourteenth century:

> The bodies seven, eek, lo heer anon.
> Sol gold is, and Luna silver we declare;
> Mars yron, Mercurie is quyksilver;
> Saturnus leed, and Jubitur is tyn,
> And Venus coper, by my father kyn.

Alchemy was deeply permeated with hylozoism, a doctrine —derived from ancient Greece and the older civilizations— that all matter is sensitive and endowed with life. Metals, like seeds (according to the mistaken medieval view), were supposed to die and undergo putrefaction before they could be revivified, ennobled, or undergo multiplication or increase. The profound belief in man's unity with nature was expressed in the common analogy which was held to obtain between the microcosm of man's body and life and the macrocosm of the outer world and the still more compre-

[1] For details see *e.g.* ref. 10 or ref. 13

hensive universe ; sometimes also an imagined alchemical microcosm crept into the scheme.

Arising from the Greek influence, alchemical beliefs were permeated with ideas inherited from the Pythagoreans. Alchemical doctrine incorporated the Pythagorean view that the cosmos originated and found its interpretation in number. The magic number 4, adopted by the Pythagoreans from earlier civilizations, held a peculiar significance as the number of the elements. The downward integral sequence from 4 is also emphasized repeatedly in alchemical writings. For example, the mysterious Basil Valentine, writing apparently at the end of the sixteenth century, stated that " all things are constituted of three essences—namely, mercury, sulphur, and salt. . . . But know that the Stone is composed out of one, two, three, four, and five. Out of five—that is the quintessence of its own substance [the Aristotelian *quinta essencia*, or ' fifth essence ']. Out of four, by which we must understand the four elements. Out of three, and these are the three principles of all things. Out of two, for the mercurial substance is twofold. Out of one, and this is the first essence of everything which emanated from the primal fiat of creation."

In a work published at Nuremberg so late as 1766, a similar idea is expressed in a table of names and corresponding symbols as shown below :

four Elements.	three Principles.	two Seeds.	one Fruit.
Fire. △			
Air. 🜁	Sulphur. 🜍	Masculine. ☉	
Water. ▽	Salt. 🜔		Tincture. ♁
Earth. 🜃	Mercury. ☿	Feminine. ☾	
from God.	from Nature.	from Metals.	from Art.

Following their observation of the existence of definite numerical relationships between the notes of musical scales, the Pythagoreans conceived the idea of a kind of celestial music, known as the music, or harmony, of the spheres, produced by the harmonic motions of heavenly bodies moving in accordance with numerical laws. It is not surprising, therefore, that some alchemists considered a musical influence to be important in their operations, particularly as music entered also so fully into the rites and ceremonies of religion, magic, and necromancy. "Joyne your Elements *Musically*," wrote Thomas Norton in 1477, on the ground that since certain "accords which in Musick be, With their proporcions causen Harmony, Much like proportions be in *Alkimy*."

The idea of the importance of music in alchemical operations reached its apotheosis in the writings of Count Michael Maier (1568–1622). Maier, a strange figure in the history of alchemy, was physician and private secretary to the Emperor Rudolph II, at Prague, a celebrated alchemical centre in the heyday of gold-makers, whose ancient habitations are still to be seen in the Zlatá Ulička, or Golden Alley. Maier's *Atalanta Fugiens* (Atalanta Fleeing), published in 1618, contains a series of fifty musical canons in two parts against a repeated *canto fermo*, to each of which is set a Latin epigram embodying an alchemical tenet or idea. A corresponding copper-engraving gives a pictorial rendering of each of the fifty themes.

Maier's writings represent also the culmination of a disposition among certain post-Renaissance alchemists to interpret classical mythology in terms of alchemy. Maier, indeed, was a leading exponent of a Hermetic mythology which was carried to extravagant lengths in the declining days of alchemy, and which finds a vivid reflection in Ben Jonson's play, *The Alchemist* (p. 39). For example, one of the engravings in *Atalanta Fugiens* (Plate 2) illustrates the mythological story of Saturn, who was given to swallowing his own offspring until foiled by Rhea's device of substituting a stone wrapped in swaddling clothes in place of the infant Jupiter. Maier's comment runs: "Wouldst thou know the reason why so many poets tell of Helicon, and why its summit is the goal of each one? There is a Stone placed on the topmost height, a memorial, which his father swallowed and spewed up instead of Jupiter . . . that Stone of Saturn is the Chymists' Stone [*i.e.* the philosopher's stone]." Medieval alchemy was permeated with a complicated Saturnine mysticism, of which more will be said later (p. 59).

Another characteristic ingredient of alchemical thought was the importance attached to colour and colour changes. In the operations of the Great Work of preparing the philosopher's stone, four principal colours were said to make their successive appearance in the order black, white, citrine, and red; these colours were also associated with the four elements and the four humours of the body (p. 58). At a certain stage in the process the colours of the peacock's tail, or of the rainbow, were supposed to make themselves evident. If the colours appeared in the wrong order the operations had to be started afresh. The re-appearance of the initial black colour at a later stage in the process was sometimes described in the cryptic alchemical phrase that the young ones of the crow were going back to their nest. The white colour was often hailed as a signal of the accomplishment of the Little Work of preparing a White Stone, capable of transmuting base metals only to the stage of silver; but the final and all-important colour, marking the completion of the Great Work or Grand Magisterium, and the attainment of the Stone or Tincture, was red: " Red is last in work of *Alkimy*," wrote Thomas Norton, the Bristol alchemist, in 1477.

Many other subsidiary ideas were pressed into the service of alchemy, a typical example being the doctrine of signatures, according to which nature was held to stamp both animate and inanimate objects with figures or shapes indicating their peculiar uses or properties. Thus the plant which the alchemists called lunary (p. 93) was supposed to draw a special virtue from the moon because of crescented markings in its leaves.

ALCHEMY AND ALCHEMISTS

Operations of the Great Work

In considering the actual operations that went forward in an alchemical laboratory it must be borne in mind that there was an esoteric alchemy, prosecuted by a closed body of adepts in accordance with the recognized doctrines of this Hermetic brotherhood, and also an exoteric alchemy conducted by uninformed "puffers," *souffleurs*, or "bellows-blowers," according to their own arbitrary ideas and whims.

The puffers, regarded by the cognoscenti as misguided "labourers in the fire," bent with bleared eyes and discoloured features over their furnaces and crucibles, in which they heated and tended strange and fantastic concoctions, after the manner of Tonsile, described in Norton's *Ordinall of Alchimy*:

> With weeping Teares he said his heart was fainte,
> For he had spended all his lusty dayes
> In fals Receipts, and in such lewde assayes ;
> Of Herbes, Gommes, of Rootes and of Grasse,
> Many kinds by him assayed was,
> As Crowefoote, Celondine, and Mizerion,
> Vervaine, Lunara, and Martagon :
> In Antimony, Arsenick, Honey, Wax and Wine,
> In Haire, in Eggs, in Merds, and Urine,
> In Calx vive, Sandifer, and Vitriall,
> In Markasits, Tutits, and every Minerall.

In the first decade of the sixteenth century the chief materials used by James IV's private alchemist, John Damian, in the royal laboratory at Stirling Castle, included alum, brimstone, cinnabar, gold, litharge, orpiment, quicksilver, red lead, sal ammoniac, saltpetre, silver, sugar, tin, verdigris, vermilion, vinegar, white lead—and large quantities of aqua vitae, "small," "ordinary," and "thrice-drawn."

To be fair, it must be said that some of the strange operations were quite logical in the light of current beliefs. For example, a metal could be killed, or submitted to mortification or putrefaction, by heating it in the air. The calx resulting from the burning, or calcination, could then be revivified or resurrected by heating it with wheat or some other living [organic] material. Here, in modern parlance, is an example of oxidation followed by the reverse process of reduction.

In general the puffers held that an initial supply of gold was necessary in gold-making, or "multiplying," in view of the dictum that bodies could multiply only in their own species. Mercenary alchemists therefore attached themselves to wealthy patrons who were willing to supply them adequately with this indispensable starting material.

To the adepts also gold was a necessity; for it was through the refining of gold by secret processes, such as solution in aqua regia, followed by crystallization (or evaporation) and calcination, that sophic sulphur was commonly sought. Other special operations on silver were supposed to lead to sophic mercury. These two "primitive materials of the Great Work," sometimes admixed with a menstruum of "our water," or of "sophic salt," often prepared from quicksilver, were finally heated in the sealed Vase of Hermes—the egg-shaped Hermetic Vessel.

The multiplicity and the sequence of operations recognized as taking place, either within or without the Hermetic Vessel, differ widely in the many obscure accounts which are diffused throughout the vast sea of alchemical writings. George Ripley (1415–90), canon of Bridlington, denoted twelve processes in the *Twelve Gates* of his celebrated work entitled *The Compound of Alchymie;* Norton outlined a scheme of fourteen processes; Paracelsus was content with seven. Ben Jonson, in his play *The Alchemist,* includes the names of "the vexations, and the martyrizations of metals in the work": these are putrefaction, solution, ablution, sublimation, cohobation, calcination, ceration, fixation, vivification, and mortification. Sometimes a scheme of twelve processes was linked with the twelve signs of the zodiac, for example, calcination with Aries (the Ram), distillation with Virgo (the Virgin), multiplication with Aquarius (the Water-carrier), and projection with Pisces (the Fishes).

A mystical element entered into the ritual of the Hermetic Vessel, which had to be carried out prayerfully under the proper astrological influences by pious operators pure in heart. The elaborate routine might last for a period of seven days, or for a philosopher's month of forty days, or even for several years. A poem in Ashmole's *Theatrum Chemicum Britannicum* (1652) states that

> The *Glasse* with the Medicine must stand in the fyre
> Forty dayes till it be Blacke in sight;
> Forty dayes in the Blacknesse to stand he will desire,
> And then forty dayes more, till itt be White,
> And thirty in the drying if thou list to doe right.

The athanor, or furnace, and the egg-shaped and hermetically sealed vessel used in these final operations of the Great Work are shown in Plate 3. On account of its shape, symbolical of fertility, the vessel was sometimes called the Philosopher's Egg. In the earlier laboratories the apparatus was very simple in design, consisting of fireclay crucibles, metal mortars, and a large variety of vessels of earthenware or glass, including particularly alembics, cucurbites, flasks, and retorts. Small flasks, known sometimes as urinals, were used a good deal. In the later laboratories distilling apparatus of increasingly efficient design became evident, as may be seen from the paintings of Teniers and other artists of the seventeenth century.

The chief agent of the alchemists was fire, and they paid particular attention to the construction of furnaces permitting of the exercise of different degrees of heat. As fuels they used wood, charcoal, peat, and coal. Bellows came greatly into play in these laboratories, for the alchemists realized that air is the "food of fire," although they did not understand why. According to Thomas Norton:

> A parfet *Master* ye maie him call trowe,
> Which knoweth his Heates high and lowe.

ALCHEMICAL EXPRESSION AND SYMBOLISM

The alchemical adepts treated their esoteric doctrines and practical operations as weighty and sacred secrets, to be maintained as a closed body of knowledge. Their " noble practise " was thus " to vaile their secrets with mistie speech," lest the clodhopper might turn from his plough and cultivate the more alluring soil of the Sages. The literature of alchemy, of which enormous accumulations have been preserved both in printed books and manuscripts, therefore abounds in cryptic expression, often to the point of unintelligibility and incoherence. The alchemists delighted also in allegory and in symbolical representations of their doctrines and ideas. In such ways they made great play with a limited stock of ideas, upon which they rang an unending series of trivial changes, both in their expressions and their imagery. It is for this reason that alchemy, which in its essentials remained extremely static through the ages, gave rise to so great and bewildering an efflorescence of literature, the extent of which may be dimly surmised from a glance at the two massive and closely printed volumes of Ferguson's classical *Bibliotheca Chemica*.[1] Trismosin, in a burst of frankness and lucidity, stated that " the noble Alchemy is to be esteemed as the gift of God ; for it is hidden mostly in manifold proverbs, figurative sayings and parables of the old Sages."

Medieval alchemy was influenced profoundly by a series of thirteen precepts, reputed to have been engraved on an Emerald Tablet found in the tomb of Hermes. These precepts, alleged to embody the fundamental secret of the Great Work, are typical examples of cryptic alchemical language. The second, third, fourth, and fifth precepts run as follows :

2 What is below is like that which is above, and what is above is like that which is below, to accomplish the miracles of one thing.

3 And as all things were produced by the one word of one Being, so all things were produced from this one thing by adaptation.

[1] Ref. 3

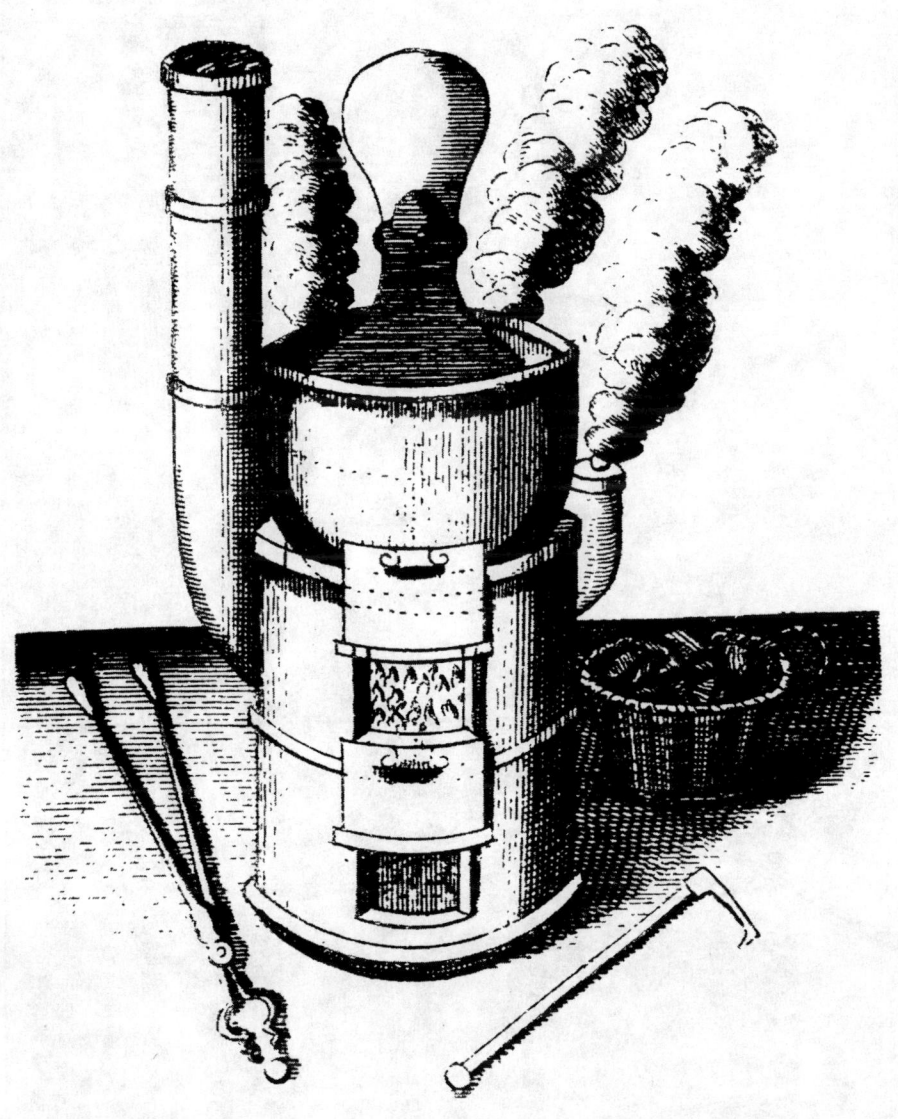

Plate 3 The Vase of Hermes in the Athanor (*page 15*)
(Barchusen)

Plate 4 The First Key of Basil Valentine (*page 19*)
(Maier)

4 Its father is the sun, its mother the moon; the wind carries it in its belly, its nurse is the earth.

5 It is the father of perfection throughout the world.

The second and third precepts embody the alchemical doctrine of the unity of all things, the fourth signifies both the primitive materials of the Great Work and the Aristotelian elements, and the fifth refers to the philosopher's stone itself.

Symbolism came into alchemy at a very early stage, and has persisted into modern chemistry, of which it is an indispensable adjunct. Among the oldest symbols of the kind are those of the sun, moon, and planets, together with the associated metals (p. 9), and also those of the four elements (p. 10). Not only the simple symbols of alchemy, but also symbolic designs of varying complexity are extremely numerous.

The important colours of alchemy often entered into alchemical drawings and paintings. A King (red) and Queen (white or blue) represented sophic sulphur and sophic mercury in esoteric alchemy, and gold and silver in exoteric alchemy. The colours of the Great Work were often represented by birds, such as the crow (black), swan (white), and phoenix (red). The formation of a white sublimate was sometimes expressed by depicting a swan or dove in upward flight. Even pieces of apparatus had their symbols, such as a bear for a still, an ostrich for a flask, and a stork for a retort.

The conjunction of the masculine and feminine principles was sometimes indicated as a hermaphroditic figure or androgyne, known as the "Rebis" or "Two-Thing." The serpent or dragon was particularly important in alchemical imagery. Winged and wingless serpents or dragons (also sometimes lions and other animals) signified the volatile and fixed principles; three serpents often represented the *tria prima*. A serpent or dragon was also used to designate a fluid menstruum which was sometimes held to be necessary to bring about the union of sophic sulphur and sophic mercury. This menstruum, under such names as "our water," "heavy water," "water not wetting the hands," or "philosophical water," was frequently depicted as a Hermetic Stream. The "heavy water" of alchemy is also bound up with the Saturn mysticism. Saturn, in the guise of an ancient wooden-legged man, or cripple, is occasionally shown in the act of watering the sun-tree and moon-tree, so as to promote multiplication of the gold and silver fruits of these alchemical trees.

Among the most famous of the medieval gold-makers was Nicolas Flamel (1330–1418), a Parisian scrivener who is said to have found the secret of the Great Work in a mysterious "guilded Booke, very old and large," with a cover "of brasse, well bound, all engraven with letters, or strange figures." These so-called "figures of Abraham the Jew" formed the subject of a series of elaborate frescoes with which Flamel decorated the arcade of the churchyard of the Innocents in Paris. The designs, appropriately coloured, were endowed with a dual alchemical and religious significance, and they gave rise to much of the symbolism of medieval alchemy. The story of Flamel and his devoted wife, Perrenelle, forms one of the most romantic of all alchemical episodes.

Another outstanding example of alchemical symbolism is to be found in a tract entitled *Splendor Solis* (Splendour of the Sun), ascribed to Salomon Trismosin. A manuscript version of this tract in the British Museum (Harley MS. 3469) contains twenty-two allegorical paintings of great interest and beauty; it bears the date 1582.

A few years later, at the opening of the seventeenth century, appeared a celebrated series of alchemical publications under the name of Basil Valentine, a reputed monk of the fifteenth century or earlier. Internal evidence points to the works having been written in the era of their publication, and they afford a striking example of the pseudepigraphic nature of a great deal of the literature of alchemy. The name Basil Valentine, meaning the "mighty King," is conceived in the true alchemical tradition. Of all the publications under this name, the emblems known as the

Twelve Keys take pride of place. This famous series of twelve symbolic designs purports to open the doors to " the most Ancient Stone of our Ancestors," and " the most secret Fountain of All Health."

The King and Queen of the First Key (Plate 4) represent Sol and Luna, or gold and silver of exoteric alchemy, and sophic sulphur and sophic mercury of the adepts. The operator is instructed to cast the body of the King to a fierce grey wolf, " and when he has devoured it, burn him entirely to ashes in a great fire. By this process the King will be liberated ; and when it has been performed thrice the Lion has overcome the wolf, who will find nothing more to devour in him. Thus our Body has been rendered fit for the first stage of our work."

These cryptic directions would lead the adept to purify gold by fusing it three times with antimony—the alchemical *lupus metallorum*, or " wolf of the metals "—in the crucible shown beneath the wolf. The ancient wooden-legged man with a scythe represents the slow-moving planet Saturn, and hence the dull, heavy metal lead. Silver, represented by the Queen, is being purified by heating it with lead in the adjacent cupel. Fire is symbolized by the scythe, the triple purification of the King (or possibly the *tria prima*) by the three flowers, and the colours of the peacock's tail by the fan. The emblem thus outlines the preparation of the " proximate materials " of the Great Work, their conjunction in the vase of Hermes being equivalent to the marriage of the King and Queen—" the faire White Woman married to the Ruddy Man," as Norton expressed it in the *Ordinall of Alchimy*.

An example of a symbolic representation of a diagrammatic character, found in writings ascribed to Basil Valentine and often associated with the emerald table of Hermes, is shown in Plate 5. Here the astrological influence exerted on the conjunction of the masculine and feminine principles, shown as sun and moon, is denoted by the symbols of the five planets, proceeding from the darkened symbol of Saturn (p. 62) to those of Mars, Venus, Jupiter, and Mercury, upon the last of which rests a cup or chalice. This symbol of fruitfulness is reminiscent of that allegorical fount of physical and spiritual life, the Holy Grail. Linked with the lion and two-headed eagle, representing the fixed and volatile principles, or sulphur and mercury, is a seven-pointed star suggestive of the correspondence between the seven metals in the earth beneath and the seven heavenly bodies in the firmament above. The double circle enclosing another group of seven objects, to the left of the star, indicates that the seven metals arise from two " seeds " (p. 10). The two hoops, to the right of the star, may be a token on the one hand of the armillary sphere, sometimes associated with Hermes, and on the other of the ancient Gnostic symbol of a snake biting its tail, conveying the ideas of rejuvenation, eternity, and the universe. The central double circle is another reminder of the dual character of metals; the orb upon which it rests is one of many symbols for the philosopher's stone. The pointing fingers are sometimes found on moon talismans. The outside square is suggestive of the four elements. The accompanying legend gives an instruction to the searcher: " Visit the inward parts of earth; by rectifying thou shalt find the hidden Stone." The Latin words form an acrostic, the initial letters being VITRIOL. Presumably, therefore, vitriol—a general term for a shiny, crystalline body—is an ingredient to be used in the processes of the Great Work.

The cult of pictorial representation in alchemy reached a climax in a strange publication at La Rochelle, in 1677, bearing the title of *Mutus Liber*. This anonymous " Wordless Book," consisting of fifteen enigmatical engravings, dispensed with words altogether, and purported to set forth " the whole of Hermetic Philosophy . . . in hieroglyphic figures, sacred to God the merciful, thrice best and greatest, and dedicated to the Sons of Art only, the name of the author being Altus."

The interest of alchemical symbolism is not confined to alchemy. As Jung has pointed out, this characteristic feature of the alchemical imagination has a profound psychological significance. Moreover it is not without importance in the realm of art. " As with any great division of human experience, alchemy is a microcosm in which the artistic trends in the greater macrocosm can be traced. For instance, in alchemical engraving, there is a slow movement from the woodcut to the copper plate and etching, and from the copper plate to the stipple engraving and mezzotint." [1]

Artistically, alchemical engravings reached their zenith in the seventeenth century, when alchemy itself was on the wane. Some of the finest productions of the kind, the work of Johannes Theodorus de Bry and his associates, are to be found in the works of Michael Maier, notably in *Atalanta Fugiens* and *Symbola Aureae Mensae*, published at Frankfurt in 1617–18. These beautifully executed copper-engravings are characterized by an intriguing blend of Gothic and Renaissance styles, as may be seen, for example, in Plate 6, from the former work. This captivating design symbolizes the heating of the Hermetic Vessel, or philosopher's egg, the alchemist being shown in the guise of one wielding a sword, symbolizing fire. He is adjured to aim at the egg " carefully, as is the custom, with the fiery sword ; let Mars [iron] lend his aid to Vulcan [fire], and thence the chick [philosopher's stone] arising will be conqueror of iron and fire."

The following comment on this design is of interest : " A strange, fanatical figure balances before the Egg, eyeing it intently and threatening it with upraised sword ; the paved court, the passage beyond, the doorway with its classical surround, might have been copied from Raphael, whilst the skyline is broken by sharp-pitched Gothic roofs and dormer windows. So insistent is the perspective that the eye is drawn to the Egg and beyond it to the distant end of the passage ; and the swordsman, for all his bulging muscles, seems dreamlike and nebulous. The engraving is reminiscent of nothing so much as one of Chirico's paintings of some empty courtyard with marble statue and cold, blue shadows ; and indeed Surrealists have lighted upon alchemical engravings with enthusiasm, finding in them the dis-

[1] J. H. Read, ref. 15

turbing and incongruous juxtapositions of their own work. ... Where the modern Surrealist repeats his sewing-machine, his umbrella, or his operating table, his predecessor, the alchemist, resorted to androgynes, to trees whose fruit was suns and moons, to Saturn with watering-pot and wooden leg, or to blind men whose lanthorns poured light across the paths they could not see. 'Is there a thing whereof men say, "See, this is new?" It hath been already, in the ages which were before us.' Modern art finds many an echo in these old engravings."

Discussing the technique of these engravings the same writer remarks: "The plates were boldly and decisively engraved with a fairly coarse burin and display considerable technical skill, together with a strong feeling for composition. Textures are well conveyed by different systems of shading; air and wind are represented by parallel curved lines; water by close parallel horizontal lines, crossed at right angles by vertical lines and broken by white patches where reflections occur; the undulations of the ground by curved, cross-hatched lines. The whole effect is enhanced by the strong modelling and shadows, and is one of brilliance and solidity. Human figures are drawn forcefully and correctly. ... In the copies of *Atalanta Fugiens* which we have examined, as also in the reprint of 1687 entitled *Secretioris Naturae Secretorum Scrutinium Chymicum*, paper and ink have remained surprisingly fresh, and the contrast between them is brilliant. The engravings balance the beautiful Roman and italic type far more successfully than do, for example, Robert Vaughan's more finely incised plates in Ashmole's *Theatrum Chemicum Britannicum* of 1652." [1]

Alchemical woodcuts and copper-engravings were intended as illustrations of the ideas and processes of alchemy rather than of the alchemists themselves, although these were occasionally shown symbolically, as in Plate 6. The central figure in Dürer's *Melencolia*, discussed below (p. 61), is perhaps the most striking of all such symbolical representations. Prominent among early realistic delineations

[1] J. H. Read, ref. 15

of an alchemist at work is a drawing in a fifteenth-century manuscript copy of Norton's *Ordinall of Alchimy*, which shows an alchemist (possibly Norton himself) seated at a table before a balance in a case.[1] Formal representations of alchemists may also be found in some of the early woodcuts of Brunschwick's *Liber de Arte Distillandi*, first published at Strassburg in 1500. A few years later came Weiditz's spirited and realistic woodcut of an alchemist and his assistant in their laboratory (p. 31), which is probably the best example of such a representation of a genuine alchemical interior of that period.

It was not until the painters, notably those of the Low Countries, turned their attention to the alchemist that justice was at last done to genre representations of a subject with such alluring possibilities: this development, of so great an interest to historical science, is dealt with in a later chapter.

Types of Alchemists

In finishing this brief sketch of a vast and complex subject, a word may be said about the alchemists themselves. It is important to regard the alchemist as a genus rather than a species. There were indeed as many kinds of alchemists as of colours in the rainbow which figured so often in their imagery. At one end of the spectrum came the mercenary impostors or charlatans, using a pretended knowledge of the " Divine Art " as a means of extracting gold of a strictly non-alchemical origin from the money-bags of credulous patrons; at the other, the devotees of a mystical alchemy played like a Maier with the ideas of Hermetic mythology, or knelt after the manner of a Khunrath in the midst of their crucibles and retorts, and murmured prayers commingling the Christian mystery of the Trinity with the alchemical mystery of the triune stone.

Between these extremes there came the simple uninformed puffers or *souffleurs*, sustained in their arduous and never-

[1] Reproduced in ref. 11

ending operations by a vivid faith in the possibility of transmutation; there came also the forerunners of the later generations of chemists, men like Brunschwick, Agricola, Libavius, and Glauber, with their absorbing interest in chemical phenomena, the discovery of new substances, and the practical application of their work in the arts; beyond these again were ranged the philosophers, like Albertus Magnus and Roger Bacon, who sought to peer beyond the experimental veil in their search for an all-embracing cosmical scheme.

To the alchemists we may apply some words of Kingsley: "Most of them were poor; many all but unknown in their time, many died and saw no fruit of their labours . . . of some the very names are forgotten." Let us despise neither their labourings nor their imaginings; for they followed, generation after generation, along a path that was destined to lead in a later age into the spacious domains of modern chemistry. To quote their own guiding motto: *Ora, lege, labora et invenies.*

Plate 5 An Emblem of the Great Work (*page 19*)
(Stolcius)

Plate 6 "Aim at this carefully with the fiery sword" (*page 21*)
(Maier)

Chapter Two

THE ALCHEMIST IN LITERATURE

Introductory

HUMAN interest, as a rule, is singularly lacking in alchemical writings. Such compositions throw little light upon the individuality of the writer or even upon his surroundings and his methods of work. There are some exceptions to this rule, and one of the most notable is provided by Thomas Norton of Bristol in his *Ordinall of Alchimy*. This attractive work, written in 1477 in rhymed English verse, tells us something of the thoughts and feelings of the writer, and describes in considerable detail the equipment, organization, and practice of his laboratory.[1]

Dating apparently from about the same period, comes also a brief but fascinating account of the wanderings and adventures of Salomon Trismosin in his search for the stone. This flowing narrative, full of verve and circumstantial detail, and related in the first person, is reputed to have been written by Trismosin himself. It appeared with *Splendor Solis* (p. 18) in a collection of alchemical tracts printed at Rorschach in 1598 and entitled *Aureum Vellus oder Guldin Schatz und Kunstkammer* (The Golden Fleece, or Golden Treasure and Art-Chamber).

The hero first took service with a miner called Flocker, who had the secret of transmuting lead into gold. He kept this secret to himself, and it disappeared abruptly with him when he had the misfortune to tumble down a mine. Then, in 1473, Trismosin set forth on his travels " to search out an artist in Alchemy." From Laibach he went on to Milan,

[1] Ref. 11

where he served for a year as an assistant in a monastery, and attended "some excellent lectures," presumably on alchemy. After travelling from place to place in Italy he worked for fourteen weeks in the employ of "an Italian tradesman and a Jew" who ran a thriving business in imitation silver, which they made from English tin. Some German assayers tested this "silver" in Venice by cupellation; "but it did not stand the test, and all flew away in the fire."

Through this circumstance Trismosin, although at first regarded with suspicion by the assayers, obtained a post as a laborant with a wealthy Venetian nobleman living in a mansion at Ponteleone. Here he worked in a well-equipped laboratory at a weekly wage of two crowns, with free board and lodging; each of the nine laborants had a private room, and there was a special cook to prepare their meals. Trismosin became acquainted with a large variety of operations in this laboratory, in which he "tinged three metals into fine gold." In all these matters he was sworn to strict secrecy. Then the Venetian nobleman, like the miner, came to a sudden end, owing to a hurricane overwhelming his pleasure ship at the ceremony of wedding the Adriatic with a gem ring.

After this, in another place, Trismosin was entrusted with cabbalistic and magical books, which were translated under his direction from the Egyptian language into Greek and Latin. There also, he "found and captured the Treasure of the Egyptians" and worked at a tincture, of which, according to his closing statement, one part could tinge 1,500 parts of silver into gold.[1]

Still later, at the opening of the seventeenth century, came the even more detailed and circumstantial account of the alchemical odyssey of Alexander Seton, the so-called "Cosmopolite," whose meteor-like career is said to have ended in tragedy at Cracow in 1604. The verisimilous accounts of successful transmutations in the Setonian epic

[1] See the anonymous English version of *Splendor Solis*, with notes, etc., by J. K., London, n.d. [1921]

are closely analogous to those occurring in the narratives of van Helmont and Helvetius, later in the seventeenth century;[1] these, in turn, are reminiscent in some respects of the equally circumstantial account (written in the first person) of the much earlier transmutations alleged to have been accomplished by Nicolas Flamel and Perrenelle his wife " in the yeere of the restoring of mankind, 1382." All such gold-making episodes are deeply tinged with an element of fantasy, and contribute little to a realistic visualization of the operations and environment of an alchemist at work.

Altogether, it is a striking fact that the most effective descriptions of alchemists and their ways of life and speech are to be found in general literature, two of the outstanding sources being Chaucer's *Canon's Yeoman's Tale* and Ben Jonson's play, *The Alchemist*.

There are many minor references in literature to the alchemist, particularly to the type who is less an alchemist than a magician, necromancer, astrologer, cheiromancer, or charlatan at large. Such characters flit occasionally across the pages of Scott, Dumas, and other romantic writers. Galeotti Marti, in *Quentin Durward* (1823), is an example of the astrological kind. Moreover, there is a distinct alchemical flavour about Dousterswivel, in *The Antiquary* (1816). This character derived from one Raspe, an able but unscrupulous chemist and mineralogist who professed in 1791 to have discovered valuable mineral deposits in the north of Scotland, and who also brought out in the same year an English translation of Baron Inigo Born's *New Process of Amalgamation of Gold and Silver Ores*. Appropriately enough, Raspe collected the marvellous stories of Baron Munchausen, which he published in 1785.

Alexandre Dumas, in *Mémoires d'un Médecin* (1846–48), exploited the famous Sicilian "alchemist" and impostor, Giuseppe Balsamo (1743–95), and his master, the Greek mystic, Althotas. Better known as "Count" Alessandro Cagliostro, Balsamo was a modern Forman (p. 47). Specializing in love-philtres, elixirs to restore youth and beauty, and

[1] Ref. 12

such-like nostrums, he amassed a considerable fortune. He was concerned in the celebrated affair of the Diamond Necklace, and ended his life in prison.

Conan Doyle's *Micah Clarke* (1888) affords still another glimpse of an alchemist who was also an astrologer. In this lively romance, Sir Jacob Clancing, the hermit of Salisbury Plain, sends the Duke of Monmouth a gift of his alchemical gold, together with the cryptic warning:

> When thy star is in trine,
> Between darkness and shine,
> Duke Monmouth, Duke Monmouth,
> Beware of the Rhine!

Had the alchemist and astrologer been a more skilful rhymester, perhaps the ill-fated duke would not have confused the German river with the Bussex Rheen of Sedgemoor!

It is surprising that in spite of his picturesque and romantic appeal, the true alchemist has figured little in literature, although slight works of minor interest may occasionally be found in which an alchemist is the chief character.[1] There is, of course, Balzac's classical *La Recherche de l'Absolu* (1834), in which Balthazar Claes is temperamentally an alchemist of the genuine type, although he falls in time outside the alchemical era. Nowhere else in literature, as Saintsbury remarks, "has the hopeless tyranny of the fixed idea, the ferocious (not exactly selfish) absorption in the pursuit of a craze, been portrayed with quite the same power as here."

Even Chaucer and Ben Jonson do not deal with full-blooded alchemists. Nevertheless, among the few convincing portraits of alchemists to be found in the literature of the nations, none is more artistic, none is more instructive, none is more racy of the alchemical soil, than are the creations of these two great English masters, sundered in time by two centuries.

---

[1] e.g. P. Ross, *A Professor of Alchemy (Denis Zachaire)*, London, 1887

THE ALCHEMIST IN LITERATURE

An Alchemist among the Canterbury Pilgrims

Geoffrey Chaucer (*c.* 1340–1400), "the father of English poetry," is famous above all as the author of the *Canterbury Tales*. Chaucer (Plate 7) was a man of many activities and interests. That he had a knowledge of the science of his day is shown by his unfinished *Treatise on the Astrolabe*, written about 1391. The *Canon's Yeoman's Tale*, one of the *Canterbury Tales* probably written in the same period, shows that Chaucer was well acquainted with the contemporary practice of alchemy and with the human traits of its practitioners. This narrative is the most charming and understanding of all accounts of alchemists and their operations that have come down to us from medieval times. Its accuracy of detail suggests that Chaucer himself had a first-hand experience of the joys and sorrows of a "labourer in the fire." The Canon of the *Tale* is an alchemist, and the Yeoman who relates most of it is his laboratory assistant, or "minister," to use Norton's term of a century later. The alchemical characters of the *Tale* are either puffers (*souffleurs*) or charlatans, and the story therefore gives the exoteric rather than the esoteric view of alchemy.

The charlatans of alchemy were mere tricksters, pure if not always simple, and as such they call for no further comment. The puffers, or bellows-blowers, however, inspire sympathy as earnest seekers after the philosopher's stone. Their unending labours, although arbitrary and uninformed, and usually actuated by sordid motives, were sustained by a fervent faith in the existence of a potent transmuting agent. In one form, as the powder of projection, they held this agent to be capable of raising imperfect base metals, through rapid and complete transmutation, to the perfection of gold; in another guise, as the Elixir of Life, they venerated it as a sovereign remedy for human ills, bringing rejuvenation and longevity in its train.

The prologue to the *Canon's Yeoman's Tale* opens on the road, with a description of the overtaking of the company of Canterbury pilgrims by the "Canoun" and his "Yeoman,"

THE ALCHEMIST IN LITERATURE

who are mounted upon horses. They have come along at a smart pace and the horses and riders alike are feeling the heat. The Canon wears black clothes, with a white robe showing underneath. His " cloke was sowed unto his hood . . . his hat heng at his back doun by a lace." Chaucer makes an early and topical jape at him : [1]

> A dock*e*-leef he had under his hood
> For sweat, and for to kepe his hed from hete.
> But it was joy*e* for to see him swete ;
> His forhed droppèd as a stillatorie.

It becomes evident forthwith that the Canon is a reputed master of the gold-making art, for the Yeoman states in introducing his lord :

> That al this ground on which we be ridynge
> Til that we come to Caunterbury toun,
> He coude al clen*e* turnen up so doun,
> And pave it al of silver and of gold.

A claim so startling evokes a forthright comment from the Host, who touches directly upon an incongruity which was too often overlooked by credulous believers in the powers of alchemy :

> His over cote it is not worth a myte
> For suche a man ; that ye may see and know
> It is al filthy and to-tore also.
> Why is thy lord so slottish, I thee preye,
> And yet hath power better clothes to buy,
> If that his might accord*e* with thy speche ?

This disconcerting query was put in various forms to alleged gold-makers seeking funds from princes and other wealthy patrons. The official reply was that gold, like everything else in nature, multiplied only in its own species. Hence in order to produce gold in quantity a certain amount

---

[1] The quotations are from the version of Chaucer's *Canterbury Tales* published in Everyman's Library, ed. A. Burrell ; italicized *e*'s and accented syllables are all sounded.

of the seed of gold, or philosopher's stone, was needed. Ordinary gold was the chief raw material requisite for the preparation of such seed. In other words, the patron of the gold-maker backed his fancy in much the same way as in a later age he would have backed a potential winner of the Derby; but with undeclared odds against him that would make a bookmaker blush. Since at the moment the Canon is not soliciting a patron, the official reply is replaced in this instance by an ingenuous substitute:

> As clerk*es* say, too much is naught at al;
> Wherfore in that a fool I may him call.
> For when a man hath over-greet a wit,
> Ful ofte him happeth to mysusen it;
> So doth my lord, and that me greveth sore.

The Host is an observant companion, and his questioning becomes still more personal when he asks the Yeoman: "Why art thou so discoloured on thy face?" As the Canon remains out of earshot, the Yeoman begins to pour out the pent-up bitterness of his soul:

> I am so usèd in the fyr to blowe,
> That it hath chaungèd al my colour I trowe;
> I am not wont in no mirour to prie,
> But labour sore, and lerne to multiplie.
> We blonder ever, and gaze into the fyr,
> And for al that we faile of oure desire,
> For ever we lacken oure conclusioun.

The picture is developing, and the bewildered Yeoman taking shape before our eyes bears a strong likeness to the figure shown in the background of Hans Weiditz's representation of an alchemist's laboratory, made about the year 1520 (Plate 8). Here also, the "filthy and to-tore" garb of the "slottish lord" at the hearth is all too evident.

The Yeoman continues his story. We learn more of the Canon. It becomes clear that his manners have not "that repose which stamps the caste of Vere de Vere" in the alchemical hierarchy. He does not belong to the inner circle of the adepts or illuminati. The religious and mystical aspects of alchemy, and the veiled secrets of the esoteric brotherhood, are to him a closed book. He is a mercenary alchemist, an exoteric gold-maker, a puffer whose sole interest in " the Divine Art " lies in the prospect of obtaining golden feathers for his own nest. He is condemned out of the mouth of his own Yeoman:

> To moche folk we bring but illusioún,
> And borrow gold, be it a pound or tuo,
> Or ten or twelve, or many somm*es* mo,
> And make them thinken at the leas*te* weye,
> That of a single pound we can make tweye.
> Yet is it fals.

The suspicious Canon now draws near and threatens to take action against the Yeoman for his 'slanderous speech. Supported by the sturdy Host, however, the Yeoman snaps his fingers at his erstwhile lord, who makes off in shamefaced confusion. The Yeoman proceeds with the substance of his tale:

> With this Canoún I duellèd have seven yer
> But to his science am I never near;
> Al that I hadde, I have y-lost therby,
> And God wot, so hath many mo than I.

After losing all his capital, and apparently working without remuneration for seven years, the ill-used Yeoman finds that the smoke and fumes of the laboratory have affected his health as well as his clothing:

> Though I was wont to be right fresh and gay
> Of clothing, and of other good array,
> Now may I were an hose upon myn heed;
> And where my colour was both fressh and red,
> Now it is wan, and of a leden hewe.

It is now fully evident what advice the narrator would give to those about to become canons' yeomen, and he summarises his experiences in the trenchant statement:

> That slippery science hath me made so bare,
> That I have no good, wher that ever I fare.

Plate 7 Geoffrey Chaucer (*page 29*)
(Occleve)

Plate 8 An Alchemist and his Assistant at Work (*page 31*)
(Weiditz)

At this point the Yeoman goes on to speak of his work, and here he spreads out before our eyes a rich array of intimate details for which we might search in vain through the great omnibus collections of formal alchemical writings. His opening remarks remind us that the vocabulary and expressions of alchemy and chemistry have always been impressive and somewhat repellent to the layman:

> Whan we be ther where we shul exercise
> Oure elvish craft, we sem*e* wondrous wyse,
> Oure term*es* be so lerned and so queynte.

Perhaps the greatest value of the Yeoman's account lies in his repeated allusions to the subjective aspect of the activities going on in his laboratory. So now, he turns suddenly from the language of alchemy to a matter of far greater personal interest to himself—namely, the bellows:

> I blowe the fyr til that myn hert*e* feynte.

A world of meaning is crystallized in this sentence of nine words. The bellows played a leading part in the operations of an alchemical laboratory, and it was for this reason that the uninformed seekers after gold were often termed puffers by the adepts. The duties of the Yeoman were largely bound up with " keeping the pot a-boiling " on the alchemical hearth.

Illustrations such as that by Weiditz (Plate 8), show that alchemical laboratories of this period resembled a blacksmith's forge in their general design. Besides the typical hearth with its ancillary bellows, they were equipped with an anvil and a selection of blacksmith's tools. The most prominent piece of alchemical apparatus in such laboratories was the croslet, or crucible, the form of which has persisted to the present day. The Yeoman mentions many other " vessels made of erthe and glas," such as urinals (small flasks), alembics (still-heads), and—as he adds scornfully— " othere suche, not worthe a green*e* leeke."

The materials, or reagents, used in the Canon's laboratory are closely similar to those described by Thomas Norton towards the end of the following century. Besides various potent herbs, among them valerian and lunary, the long list includes silver, quicksilver, orpiment, sal ammoniac, brimstone, quicklime, chalk, egg-white, dung, saltpetre, alum, argol, and less definite materials such as " cley made with hors or mannes hair."

As in the modern laboratory, unfortunate occurrences were not infrequent in that alchemical laboratory of some six hundred years ago. Sometimes, as the Yeoman observes, the reactants " be of so gret violence, Oure walles may not make them résistence." The result is familiar. Then, as now, one had to accept the principle of the inherent malignity of matter and to take risks with apparatus:

> And wit ye how? ful ofte it happeth so,
> The pot to-breketh, and farwel, al is go . . .
> There never was suche wo or anger or ire
> As when oure pot is broke, as I have sayd,
> Every man chideth, and thinketh him ill paid.
> Som sayd it was too long on the fyr-makyng;
> Some sayde nay, it was on the blowyng;
> (Than was I feard, for that was myn office).

The human element in alchemy has never been depicted more vividly than in these eloquent words. All of us can understand the feelings, if not the language, of the dismayed workers as they gaze in consternation and disgust at their scattered " yields." To do him justice, the Canon steps manfully into the breach and pours all the available oil on the troubled waters:

> " What? " quoth my lord, " ther is no more to doon,
> Of these periles I wil be ware eftsoon.
> I am right certeyn, that the pot was crasèd.
> Be as be may, be ye no thing amasèd.
> As usage is, let swoope the floor up soon;
> Pluk up your hertes and be glad and boon."

It is not easy to be " glad and boon " in such circumstances, but the laboratory staff grasp their dustpans and brooms and turn to with a will, for " the remnaunt on an heep i-swopèd was." In other words, the shards are swept up, and everything possible is done to recover the residues, which are gathered on a piece of canvas and shaken through a sieve; so in this way is " y-plukkèd many a throwe." A more optimistic spirit begins to prevail:

> " In faith," quoth one, " somwhat of oure metal
> Yet is ther heer, though that we have nought al.
> And though this thing myshappèd hath as now,
> Another tyme it may be wel y-now."

This speaker goes on to emphasize the importance of enterprise in research. One must learn to cast one's bread upon the waters. It is not reasonable to expect a theoretical yield from every experiment:

> " Us moste putte oure good in áventúre.
> A marchaunt, truly, may not ay endure,
> Truste me wel, in his prosperitee,
> Som tyme his good is drownèd in the see,
> And som tyme cometh it sauf unto the londe."

So " atte last " the incident is composed, and the laboratory staff settle down to work again. We all feel that we have been there too—"ful many a tyme and ofte."

Throughout the narrative, although it is clear that the Canon has not come out of the alchemical top-drawer, yet we have heard of no deliberate deception on his part. He is an uninformed labourer in the fire, a simple puffer in his flower, who deceives and beggars himself as well as his clients in his hopeful efforts to achieve multiplication.

Now, however, in the second part of the *Tale*, we come to a black page in the Yeoman's narrative. He turns to an account of the activities of another Canon:

> That can an hundred fold more subtiltee.
> He hath bitrayèd folkes many a tyme;
> Of his falsness it dullith me to ryme.
> And ever when I speke of his falshede,
> For shame of him my cheekes wexen red.

This "alchemister" entered into relationships with a priest whose confidence he gained by means of a series of rigged experiments. The Yeoman's circumstantial account of these alleged transmutations stamp this second Canon as a charlatan, impostor, and cheat.

In his first demonstration the Canon "took out a crosselett, out of his bosom, and shewed it to the priest." He then invited his prospective victim to walk up the garden path, along the primrose way of his secret philosophy, adding that there were "ful fewe" to whom he was prepared to show so much of his science:

> "This instrument," quoth he, "which that thou seest,
> Tak in thin hond, and put thiself therinne
> Of this quyksilver an ounce, and here bygynne
> In the name of Crist to wax a philosophre."

The Canon then produced a small specimen of his infallible transmuting powder, or philosopher's stone, with the remark, "I have a powder here that cost me deere"; upon which expensive preparation the Yeoman makes the pulverizing comment:

> A powder, I knew not wherof it was
> I-made, either of chalk, either of glas,
> Or som what else, that was nought worthy a flye.

The Canon then cast some of his powder of projection into the crucible already charged with the ounce of quicksilver, and invited the priest to arrange the vessel in the charcoal fire. Having thus distracted the attention of his dupe,

> This false canoun (the foule feend him fetche !)
> Out of his bosom took a false cole,
> In which ful subtilly was made an hole,
> And therin was put of silver metál
> An ounce, and stoppèd was withoute fayle
> This hole with wax, to kepe the metal in.

Meanwhile the priest had become heated with his exertions at the hearth, and the wily Canon handed him a cloth with the disarming remark, "Ye be right hot, I see wel how ye swete." Whilst the unsuspecting priest proceeded to "wype away the wete," the Canon deftly inserted the doctored piece of charcoal among the other fuel in a favourable position above the crucible, and plied the bellows with vigour. In due course the molten silver ran down and collected on the floor of the crucible, thus creating the impression that the original quicksilver—now completely lost by volatilization—had been transmuted into an equal weight of silver.

The Canon, who seems to have graduated with high honours in conjuring, carried out other "cooked experiments" of a similar kind, in which he concealed the silver in his sleeve, or in a hollow stirring rod closed with wax:

> He styred the col*es*, til to melt began
> The wex agaynst the fyr, as every man,
> But it a fool be, wot wel that it doth,
> And al that in the hol*e* was out goth,
> And into the croslet hastily it fel.
> Now, good*e* sirs, what wil ye better than wel?

At the end of these uniformly successful demonstrations the priest asked anxiously, "What shal this réceyt cost*e*? telle me now." In apologizing for its expensive nature the Canon pointed out that "save I and a freere, In Eng*e*lond ther can no man it make." Further pressure from the priest, now becoming importunate in his newly awakened greed, at last induced the Canon to make him a quotation for the secret.

> "I-wis," quoth he, "it is ful dere I say.
> Sir, at a word, if that ye lust it have,
> Ye shul paye fourty pound, so God me save;
> And but for frendshipe that ye dede ere this
> To me, ye shulde pay*e* more, i-wys."

The priest closed eagerly with this offer, the bargain was clinched, and the two actors in this alchemical drama went away happy, the Canon with his "somme of fourty pound of nobles," and the priest with "this cursèd receyt," as the Yeoman pungently terms it. The Yeoman outlines the sequel in words few in number but well chosen :

> He went his way, and never the prest him sey
> After this day ; and when this prest sholde
> Maken assay, at such tyme as he wolde,
> Of this receyt, far wel, it wold not be.

At the end of his narrative the Yeoman makes his only reference to alchemical theory, quoting " Arnold of the Newe-toun " (Arnold of Villanova) and Hermes. According to the Yeoman, Hermes was the first to lay down the principle that the dragon could not die (undergo fixation) unless slain with his brother,

> By the dragoun, Mercúry, and noon other
> He understood, and brimstoon be his brother,
> That out of Sol and Luna were i-drawe.

This is the exoteric point of view of the unsophisticated puffer. The Yeoman takes mercury and sulphur at their face value ; he does not look beyond quicksilver and brimstone to the sophic mercury and sophic sulphur of the cognoscenti. He points out, indeed, in his simple-minded way, that " philosophres speken so mistyly in this craft, that men conne not come therby " ; nevertheless, anybody who meddles with this art, unless he can understand the language and ideas of the philosophers, is a foolish man, whose " thrift is gon ful clene." As for the philosopher's stone, the honest Yeoman ends :

> Than thus conclude I, since God on high
> Wil not that philosóphres signify,
> How that a man shal come unto this stoon,
> I counsel for the beste, let it goon.

An Alchemist in Jacobean London

A very famous presentment of an "alchemist" in English literature is that of Ben Jonson (Plate 9) in his comedy *The Alchemist* (Plates 10 and 11). This was first acted in 1610, in early Jacobean London. Unfortunately for the reputation of alchemists and alchemy, the central figure is not a true alchemist. To use the author's own words, Subtle is a "cheater" and "coz'ner at large," who conducts his nefarious practices behind a smoke-screen of alchemical verbiage. It has been suggested that Jonson was influenced by Chaucer's *Canon's Yeoman's Tale* in writing this play; but, in detail, there is little in common between the Canon and Subtle on the one hand, and the Yeoman and Face on the other. Although unfortunate in his operations, the first Canon of the *Tale* was an alchemist in spirit if not in accomplishment, a laborant as well as a bookman, and the Yeoman had spent seven arduous years in graduating as a labourer in the fire. There is little evidence in Jonson's play that, as alchemists, Subtle and Face were anything more than cross-talk artistes using the vocabulary of alchemy as their medium.

The Alchemist[1] scored an immediate success in the London of James I, and proceeded on its triumphant course when the theatres came into their own again at the Restoration. Its praise has echoed down to us through the intervening centuries. Samuel Pepys described it in 1661 as "a most incomparable play," and went to see it time and again. Coleridge considered the *Œdipus Tyrannus*, *The Alchemist*, and *Tom Jones* "the three most perfect plots ever planned." Swinburne regarded *The Alchemist* as unique and "the greatest of comic triumphs ever accomplished."

Fundamentally, Jonson's masterpiece constituted a vehement and most successful attack on the atmosphere of imposture and fraud which prevailed in early Jacobean London. It pilloried an order of things which has long since passed away, and its satiric barbs and punning allusions were framed for audiences well versed in the imagery

[1] Ref. 7

of alchemy and familiar with the alchemical vocabulary. It was written to appeal to a world that had a first-hand knowledge of such notorious practitioners in magic and pseudo-alchemy as Dr. John Dee and Simon Forman; to a world that had heard of the alchemical glories of the court of the Emperor Rudolph II and his Zlatá ulička (Golden Lane, or Street of the Alchemists) in far-away Zlatá Praha (Golden Prague). But those "happy days in fair Aranjuez are past and gone."

Nevertheless, *The Alchemist* still deserves to be read by lovers of chemistry and acted by lovers of the drama. It may be adventured with success, provided only that both actors and audience enter into the spirit of Sir Epicure Mammon's opening admonition:

> Come on, sir. Now, you set your foot on shore
> In *novo orbe*; here's the rich Peru!
> And there, within, sir, are the golden mines,
> Great Solomon's Ophir!

The golden mines are "rare Ben's" superb craftsmanship, his faultless artistry, and his masterly characterization, seasoned with dazzling wit and interspersed with a wealth of deliciously ludicrous situations. His lavish transmutation of alchemical imagery and expressions in this Great Work of English literature envelops the play in a poetic web of great beauty; at the same time, his command of these alchemical technicalities is so consummate that *The Alchemist* is one of the best and most accurate repositories of the ideas and vocabulary of seventeenth-century alchemy.

The scene of the play is Lovewit's house in London, which has been temporarily abandoned by its master because of the plague. His butler, Jeremy, who has been left as caretaker, becomes associated with Subtle, a reputed alchemist, and his female companion. "While there dies one a week o' the plague, he's safe, from thinking toward London," says Jeremy, of Lovewit. With this consideration in mind, he takes Subtle and Dol Common into the house; goes into partnership with them, under the name of Face,

Plate 9 Ben Jonson (*page 39*)
(Honthorst)

THE ALCHEMIST IN LITERATURE

as Subtle's nominal assistant; and helps them to turn the house into a thieves' kitchen. So, in Jonson's words:

> Much company they draw, and much abuse,
> In casting figures, telling fortunes, news,
> Selling of flies,[1] flat bawdry with the stone;
> Till it, and they, and all in fume are gone.

The operations of this rogues' syndicate cover so wide a field that many of their victims are not interested in alchemy at all. Thus in Act I, Abel Drugger, the tobacco-man, who is about to open a new shop, comes to ask Subtle's advice:

Drugger And I would know by art, sir, of your worship,
Which way I should make my door, by necromancy,
And where my shelves; and which should be for boxes,
And which for pots. I would be glad to thrive, sir.

Somewhat later, he adds: "Look over, sir, my almanack, and cross out all my ill-days, that I may neither bargain, nor trust upon them."

Abel Drugger, a minor character in the play, was immortalized by David Garrick, through his new and vivid interpretation of the part at Drury Lane in 1742–43. Zoffany's striking picture of a scene from *The Alchemist* depicts Garrick in this role (Plate 12). The psychological moment having arrived for Drugger to offer a suitable fee to Subtle, the latter exclaims flatteringly to "Captain" Face:

Subtle This fellow, captain,
Will come, in time, to be a great distiller,
And give a 'say (I will not say directly,
But very fair) at the philosopher's Stone.

Apart from Subtle and Face themselves, the chief exponent of alchemy in the play is Sir Epicure Mammon, their leading dupe. In the second act (Plate 11), which is particularly concerned with alchemy, Pertinax Surly, a gamester, takes his stand as a sceptical critic of alchemy and all its ideas and works. Subtle—that "smoky persecutor of nature," as Face

[1] Familiar spirits

calls him—is, in Mammon's eyes, "an excellent Paracelsian." There is no doubt that he is a master of the terminology of alchemy, but beyond this he shows little claim to be called an alchemist. He does not even attempt the experimental chicanery of Chaucer's second Canon. He is an adept in the ramifications of roguery—not in alchemy.

Face, so sly, and so nimble of wit and tongue, resembles Subtle in his word-perfect acquaintance with alchemy. Witness the *tour de force* designed to convince the Puritan deacon from Amsterdam:

Subtle Sirrah my varlet, stand you forth, and speak to him
      Like a philosopher: answer in the language,
      Name the vexations, and the martyrizations
      Of metals in the work.
Face   Sir, putrefaction,
      Solution, ablution, sublimation,
      Cohobation, calcination, ceration, and
      Fixation . . .
Subtle And whence comes vivification?
Face   After mortification.
Subtle What's cohobation?
Face   'Tis the pouring on
      Your *aqua regis*, and then drawing him off
      To the trine circle of the seven spheres.

And much more to the same effect.

The characters of Subtle and Face may have been a reflection of Dr. Dee and his associate, Edward Kelly, whose deeds and deaths were fresh in men's memories at the time when Jonson was writing the play. Alchemy was essentially experimental; but neither Subtle nor Face is presented as an active laborant. In the words of Paracelsus: "They carried golden mountains in their head before they had put their hand to the fire." It is true that Face talks to Mammon of his "bleared eyes" and exclaims:

                      I have blown, sir,
Hard for your worship; thrown by many a coal,
When 'twas not beech; weighed those I put in, just,
To keep your heat still even.

Even if this statement be taken at its Face value, this Firedrake, Lungs, or Zephyrus, as Mammon calls him, has only been at the game for a few weeks. In spite of such asseverations, Subtle and Face are but shadow alchemists, each having a retentive memory and a power of assimilating phrases, coupled with a robot-like acquaintance with certain manual operations; but, after all, their counterparts in these respects may not be unknown among modern students of chemistry.

The magniloquent Mammon is obsessed with the power of the philosopher's stone as a transmuting and rejuvenating agent. "This is the day I am to perfect for him," says Subtle,

> The magisterium, our great work, the stone:
> And yield it, made, into his hands: of which
> He has, this month, talked as he were possessed.

He interlards his survey of the approaching millennium—when (among more questionable activities) he'll "change all that is metal" in his house to gold—with classical allusions that would have delighted Count Michael Maier if he had happened to witness the play during his visit to England soon after its first performance:

> And they are gathered into Jason's helm,
> (The alembic), and then sowed in Mars his field,
> And thence sublimed so often, till they're fixed.
> Both this, th' Hesperian garden, Cadmus' story,
> Jove's shower, the boon of Midas, Argus' eyes,
> Boccace his Demogorgon, thousands more,
> All abstract riddles of our stone.

Ben Jonson's remarkable book-knowledge of alchemy, with its bewildering vocabulary, its wealth of imagery, its metaphoric expressions and classical allusions, is displayed with dazzling effect in the utterances of Subtle, Face, and Mammon. "Without sacrificing a single sordid trait in his picture of the alchemist, Jonson contrives to keep before us the visionary poetry of which, for its loftier practisers,

THE ALCHEMIST IN LITERATURE

alchemy was the expression."[1] He seems also to have had more than a nodding acquaintance with some of the practical operations of an alchemical laboratory:

Subtle   Ulen Spiegel!
Face   Anon, sir.
Subtle   Look well to the register,
And let your heat still lessen by degrees,
To the aludels.
Face   Yes, sir.
Subtle   Did you look
O' the bolt's-head yet?
Face   Which? On D, sir?
Subtle   Aye.
What's the complexion?
Face   Whitish.
Subtle   Infuse vinegar,
To draw his volatile substance and his tincture.
And let the water in glass E be filtered,
And put into the gripe's-egg. Lute him well:
And leave him closed *in balneo*.

It is often supposed that the action of *The Alchemist* takes place in an alchemical laboratory; but this is not so. The laboratory remains off-stage, and so do all the practical operations to which the characters make reference. Indeed, as the play progresses, one becomes more and more sceptical about the existence of any laboratory or any practical operations at all, except in the fertile imaginations of Subtle and Face. The progress of the alleged laboratory operations is reported by Face, who makes periodical visits behind the scenes in order to inspect the hypothetical bolt's-heads, crosslets, cucurbites, retorts and pelicans, and to regulate the furnaces and baths:

Mammon   Is it, my Zephyrus, right?
Blushes the bolt's-head? . . .
                                    And, lastly,
Thou hast descried the flower, the *Sanguis Agni*?

[1] C. H. Herford

THE ALCHEMIST.

VVritten
by
BEN. IONSON.

———*Neque, me vt miretur turba, laboro:*
Contentus paucis lectoribus.

LONDON,
Printed by *Thomas Snodham*, for *Walter Burre*,
and are to be sold by *Iohn Stepneth*, at the
West-end of Paules.
1612.

Plate 10   Title-page of the first edition of *The Alchemist* (page 39)
(London, 1612)

The ALCHEMIST.

SVB. Sonne, be not hasty, I exalt our *Med'cine*,
By hanging him in *Balneo Vaporoso*;
And giuing him solution; then *congeale* him,
And then *dissolue* him; then againe *congeale* him;
For looke, how oft I iterate the worke,
So many times, I adde vnto his vertue.
As, if at first, one Ounce conuert a hundred,
After his second loose, he'll turne a thousand;
His third solution, ten: his fourth a hundred.
After his fifth, a thousand thousand Ounces
Of any imperfect mettall, into pure
Siluer, or Gold, in all examinations,
As good, as any of the naturall Mine.
Get you your stuffe here, against afternoone,
Your Brasse, your Pewter, and your Andirons.
MAM. Not those of iron? SVB. Yes. You may bring them, too.
We'll change all mettall's. SVR. I beleeue you, in that.
MAM. Then I may send my Spitts? SVB. Yes, and your Racks.
SVR. And Dripping-pannes, and Pot-hangers, and Hookes?
Shall he not? SVB. If he please. SVR. To be an Asse.
SVB. How Sir! MAM. This Gent'man, you must beare withall.
I told you, he had no faith. SVR. And little hope, Sir,
But, much lesse charitie, should I gull my selfe.
SVB. Why what haue you obseru'd, Sir, in our Art,
Seemes so impossible? SVR. But your wholeworke, no more.
That, you should hatch gold in a Fornace, Sir,
As they doe egges in *Egypt*. SVB. Sir, doe you
Beleeue that egges are hatch'd so? SVr. If I should?
SVB. Why, I thinke that the greater Miracle.
No Egge, but differs from a Chicken, more,
Then *Mettalls* in themselues. SVR. That cannot be.
The *Egg's* ordain'd by *Nature*, to that end:
And is a Chicken, in *Potentia*.
SVB. The same we say of Lead, and other Mettalls,
Which would be Gold, if they had time. MAM. And that
Our Art doth furder. SVB. I, for 'twere absurd

E   To

Plate 11   A page from the first edition of *The Alchemist* (page 39)
(London, 1612)

Face　　　　Yes, sir.
Mammon　　　　　　Where's master?
Face　　　　　　　　　　　At his prayers, sir; he,
　　　　Good man, he's doing his devotions
　　　　For the success.

It seems strange that Mammon should not be taken into the laboratory to watch the progress of the Great Work which he is subsidizing so handsomely—to see with his own eyes the glories of the blushing bolt's-head, " the pale citron, the green lion, the crow, the peacock's tail, the plumèd swan," and the wonderful spectacle of the *Sanguis Agni*, the glorious red colour signifying the achievement of the Great Work; but doubtless he has been told that whoso approaches the Hermetic Vessel in the hour of generation of the stone must be " *homo frugi*, a pious, holy, and religious man, one free from mortal sin, a very virgin." It is fairly obvious at the outset of the play, and crystal clear towards its end, that such a characterization is far from applying to Mammon. Eventually, in the fourth act, Subtle and Face skilfully evade their obligations to that incarnation of gluttony and greed by taking advantage of a lapse from the canons of moral conduct into which they have previously lured him.

At the propitious moment Subtle enters with the announcement that the Great Work " has stood still this half hour: and all the rest of our less works gone back." He reproaches Mammon, " for whom the blessing was prepared," for so tempting heaven and risking the loss of his fortunes:

Subtle　　　　　　　　　　　This will retard
　　　　The work, a month at least.
Mammon　　　　　　　　　　　Why, if it do,
　　　　What remedy? but think it not, good father:
　　　　Our purposes were honest.
Subtle　　　　　　　　　　　As they were,
　　　　So the reward will prove. How now? ah me!
　　　　　　　[*A great crack and noise within*]
　　　　God and all saints be good to us! What's that?
　　　　　　　　　Enter Face
Face　　　　O sir, we are defeated! all the works

> Are flown *in fumo*, every glass is burst !
> Furnace and all rent down ! as if a bolt
> Of thunder had been driven through the house.
> Retorts, receivers, pelicans, bolt-heads
> All struck in shivers ! help, good sir ! alas !
>
> [Subtle *falls down in a swoon*]

Face exclaims that his " brain's quite undone with the fumes," but recovers in time to reply to Mammon's anxious query: " Is all lost, Lungs ? will nothing be preserved, of all our cost ? " " Faith, very little, sir. A peck of coals or so, which is cold comfort, sir." Subtle " seems to come to himself " with the despairing cry : " Oh, the curst fruits of vice and lust ! " After inducing Mammon to subscribe a hundred pounds to a home for the feeble-minded, as a kind of propitiatory retaining fee for anything that may yet come out of the experiments, Face shows him to the door, with an expression of the consoling possibility :

> There will be, perhaps,
> Something about the scraping of the shards
> Will cure the itch—though not your itch of mind, sir !
> It shall be saved for you, and sent home. Good sir,
> This way.

Face greets his departure with the exclamation, " Let us be light " ; and Subtle, leaping up, responds gleefully : " Aye, as balls, and bound and hit our heads against the roof for joy : there's so much of our care now cast away." The alchemical interest fades at this point. The unexpected return of Lovewit brings the play to a close in a welter of high comedy, as in quick succession the best-laid schemes of the plotters gang a-gley, recoiling upon their heads like the young ones of the crow going back to their nest when the Great Work takes an unfavourable turn.

So, summing up the play from the alchemical point of view, we are left with the impression voiced by Surly :

> That Alchemy is a pretty kind of game,
> Somewhat like tricks o' the cards, to cheat a man
> With charming.

But that is not a true appraisement of the real alchemy.

THE ALCHEMIST IN LITERATURE

An Alchemist Tells of Himself

The Alchemist was written as a critical satire upon a marked phase of London life at the opening of the seventeenth century. There is no doubt that Jonson based the characters of Subtle and Face upon certain reputed alchemists of that time and place. Of these, the three most likely prototypes are John Dee, Edward Kelly, and Simon Forman (Plate 13). Forman (1552–1611), alone of the three, was alive when the play was written, and he is mentioned by name as a concoctor of love-philtres in Jonson's play *Epicoene*, which immediately preceded *The Alchemist*. It was an age in which quack doctors, astrologers, magicians, and fortune-tellers were wont to assume the respectable and impressive title of alchemist in order to invest their calling with a show of knowledge and authority. In the invented character of Subtle we perceive a refined and caricatured likeness of such a real person as Forman. But Forman was more than an artist's model: he was a typical product of an age that witnessed the decline and debasement of alchemy, as it stood hesitatingly upon the threshold of chemistry, and as such he is worthy of more than a passing mention.

In the archives of alchemy it is exceptional to find an alchemist leaving behind him any record of his career and operations in the intimate form of a personal diary. Certainly there are alchemical episodes written in the first person, such as the fascinating narratives ascribed to Nicolas Flamel and Salomon Trismosin, and also to Dienheim, van Helmont, and Helvetius;[1] but some of them are of doubtful authenticity and none of them gives the intimate subjective impression of the day-by-day entries of a diarist. Simon Forman, however, may be visualized objectively, from contemporary references to his life and career, and also subjectively from his autobiography and personal diary.[2] It is seldom possible to compare so closely the rarefied vision of an imaginative writer like Ben Jonson with factual impressions of these two kinds.

[1] Ref. 12
[2] Ref. 4

The objective picture of Simon Forman shows him as a charlatan who claimed to be an alchemist, astrologer, magician, and seer. He studied for a short time at Oxford, visited Holland, and practised in London as a physician. Being technically unqualified, he was repeatedly fined and imprisoned for quackery, until eventually he obtained a diploma from Cambridge. He established himself at Lambeth and gradually attracted a large following, especially among society ladies interested in various aspects of matrimony.

His most celebrated association of this kind was with the notorious Countess of Essex, through the intermediary of Mrs. Turner, a gentlewoman of "a loose kind of life." This "ancient gentleman, thought to have skill in the magick-art," as Forman is described in a document [1] of 1643, wrought mightily for the countess (who addressed him as "sweet father") with "pictures in wax, crosses, and many strange and uncouth things," including an enchanted nutmeg. The aim of all this was to "inchant viscount Rochester's affection towards her" and turn her husband's away from her. This tangled affair led in 1615 to a *cause célèbre* in English history, namely, the trial of the Earl of Somerset (formerly Viscount Rochester) and his countess (formerly the Countess of Essex), with certain accomplices, for the poisoning of Sir Thomas Overbury, an inveterate opponent of his friend Rochester's marriage. Although Forman's activities had been completely innocuous, and limited to his feeble attempts at enchantment, there can be little doubt that but for his death in the meantime (1611) he would have been arraigned among the accomplices, who were all hanged. Forman's alleged powers were taken very seriously by his contemporaries. Thus in Richard Niccols' wearisome poem, *Sir Thomas Overbury's Vision*, published in 1616, he is designated as "Forman, that cunning exorcist."

> Where Lambeth's town to all well known doth stand :
> There Forman was, that fiend in human shape,
> That by his art did act the devil's ape.

[1] Reprinted in *The Harleian Miscellany*, ref. 17

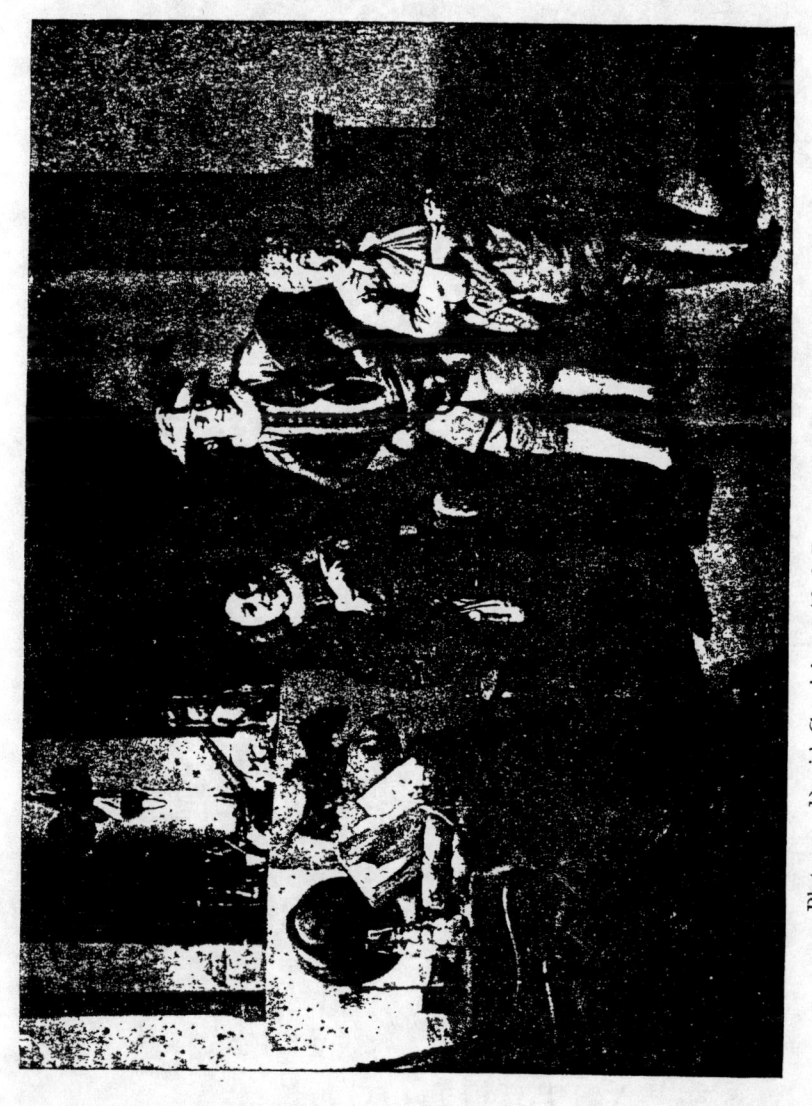

Plate 12 David Garrick as Abel Drugger in *The Alchemist* (*page 41*)
(Zoffany)

"This fellow, captain,
Will come, in time, to be a great distiller."

Plate 13 Simon Forman (*page 47*)
(Bulfinch)

That the objective view of Forman held by his contemporaries flattered enormously his attainments and powers is soon evident from a glance at the subjective picture afforded by his autobiography and personal diary. Here he is revealed as not less credulous and superstitious than his deluded clients. At the same time he is endowed with vanity and a considerable belief in his powers as a physician, seer, and necromancer. That he had little claim to the title of alchemist [1] is clear from his own record of his dabblings in the simple practical operations of alchemy; that he was equally ineffective as a magician is shown by the unending chronicle of distressing events that seemed to accompany him like an aura of misfortune. In spite of his portentous enchantments and spells, his magic ring, and his potent love-philtres for which he acquired so great a reputation among the fine ladies of his day, he appears to have had little control over his own womenfolk. His dabblings in magic and necromancy, judging by results, were no whit less futile than his philtres and his dilettantish attempts to achieve the philosopher's stone. No discerning reader of his personal diary could accept Richard Niccols' distorted view of Forman as a "fiend in human shape."

Forman's brief diary runs from 1564 to 1602. In 1600 he wrote a short autobiography of an unusual type, in which he makes himself the hero of a narrative strongly reminiscent in style and form of a black-letter prose romance. This opens as follows:

In Dei nomine, Amen. This is the bocke of the life and generation of Simon ... Forman ... borne in the yeare from the Nativity of our Lord Jesus Christ 1552, the 30. of December, beinge Saturday and new yere's eve, at 45 minutes after 9 of the clocke at nighte ... in a village called Quidhampton, in the countie of Wilts, sytuate in the valley on the north side of the river betwene Wilton and Sarum.

The close attention to date and time is a sign of the writer's deep interest in astrology: he cannot even fall

[1] He must be credited, however, with the melancholic temperament and saturnine cast of countenance appropriate to a devotee of alchemy (p. 61)!

downstairs (in which pastime he seems to have specialized), or hit his " right kne againste the dore post going forth," without noting the day and time of the occurrence.

After giving some family details, Forman proceeds to tell *Of visions that the said Symon had, beinge yet a childe*: these visions (dreams) " God did showe him in his youth, to signifie unto him his trobles in his riper years." Going on to relate *Howe Simon was set to scole, with whom and wher*, he describes a singular economy practised at Salisbury by Mr. Mintorne, a canon of the church :

And this cannon seldom or never kepte any fier in his house, but he had some lode of faggots lying in a house, and alwaies when he was a-cold, he wold goe and carry his faggots up into a lofte till he was hote ; and when he had caried them all up, he wold fetch them downe again and burn none, and soe he made this Simon doe many a tyme and ofte to catch a heate, saying yt was better to heat himself soe then to syt by the fier.

The story goes on to tell *Howe Symon after his fathers death was put to shifte for himselfe, and went to dwell with his aunte for two years*. In 1567, at the age of 14, he became apprentice to Mathewe Comins of Sarum, a man of many occupations from whom Simon learnt much :

Firste he [Simon] was a hosier, and therby he lerned to sowe and to make a hose ; then he was a merchante of cloth, and of alle smalle wares, and sold hops, salte, oille, pitch, rosine, raisons, and all poticary drugs and grocery, wherby the said Simon learned the knowledge of alle wares and drugs, and howe to buy and selle, and grue so apte, and had such good fortune, that in shorte tyme his master committed all to his charge.

However, a fly duly appeared in the ointment, in the shape of a truculent kitchen maid ; and the next two episodes are headed *Howe Symon beate Mary Robartes, his masters maide*, and *Of the quandary and fear that Simon was in when he had beaton Marie*. Fortunately, when his master returned home and found the maid " cryinge and howlinge " he was able to endorse Simon's action : " Thou servedst her well ynough, said he, and yf she be soe obstinate serve her soe again, said he"; but when his mistress returned a little later " she grudged at him moch." Anyhow, the shrew was tamed, and " after this Simon and Marie agreed soe well that they never were at square after."

Two other flies soon appeared in the ointment, the next heading being: *Of the combate betwen Simon and the too Godfries*. These two boys gave Simon hard words, and said they would have him by the ears. " Soe to buffets they wente. And Simon beate them bothe . . . and after that, Simon would not shrinke for a bluddi nose with any boye."

Since only the brave deserve the fair, the victor's prowess leads on naturally to an ingenuous account of *How A. Y. loved Simon*. Here it must be remarked that the gallant Simon adopted from this early entry the discreet practice of referring to certain of his lady admirers by their initials only. A. Y. was a " proper fine maiden . . . but yonge of yeares and younger then Simon, that loved Simon wonderfull welle, and wold suerly see him once a daie, or ells she wold be sicke." Simon, however, at this time could only promise to be a brother to her; " he loved her not but in kindnes, but because she was soe kind to Simon, he wold doe anythinge he could doe for her."

Simon's mistress had viewed him with a jaundiced eye since the beating of the kitchen wench, and it comes as no surprise that the next act in the drama shows *Howe Simon and his mistres fell at controversy, whereupon Simon at seventeen yeres old and a halfe wente from his master*. The mistress was a virago from whom both Simon and his master recoiled. In private, the master commiserated with his apprentice: " Simon, thou moste suffer as well as I myselfe"; but since in public he beat him " for his mistres sake, herselfe being in faulte, Symon told his said master flate that he had not performed his covenantes." He therefore claimed his indenture and departed, " at the which his mistres toke on mightily."

The rest of this entertaining narrative describes: *Howe Simon, after he was gone from his said master, became a scoller again at the fre scole ; Howe Simon became a scolmastre before he was eighteen yers old*; and *Howe Simon with on of his old scollefellowes wold goe seek out Oxford*. This brings the autobiography to an end, in the year 1573.

From the diary it is clear that Simon led an exiguous existence as a teacher from the time of his leaving Oxford, in 1574, until 1579. The entries for 1579 contain the first reference to his frequent imprisonments, and also the earliest indication of his coming reputation as a seer.

This yere I did profecie the truth of many thinges which afterwardes cam to passe, and the very sprites wer subjecte unto me ; what I spake was done. And I had a great name, yet I could doe nothinge, but at adventure.

In 1580, although he had command of the sprites and what he spake was done, he was in prison until 14th July; on the 18th "a cosoning quen" professed herself to be his sister ; on the 26th he went to Greenwich as a carpenter; on 16th August he visited London " to cuer Henry Jonson of a consumption " ; on 4th September he left with his patient for a month in Holland ; on 8th October he was at Newbury ; and on 18th November he returned to Quidhampton. After these varied experiences he remained at Quidhampton for nearly a year, "curing sick and lame folks " and also a victim of the king's evil. His interest in healing is shown further in the last entry for 1581 : "The 21st of October I tok a house in Sarum on the dich by the skinner, and ther I dwelte practising phisick and surgery, and I began againe to live."

The first entry of alchemical interest occurs in 1585, after Forman had been living for about two years in London : " The first of March I began to distill *aqua vitae*." This year and the next were marked by continual imprisonments, disputes, and lawsuits, creating the general impression that the diarist was apt to be quarrelsome and cantankerous. In 1587, he " began to distill many waters " on 11th May. As usual, this year also he " had moch troble and imprisonments." He adds : " I practised magik, and had moch strife with divers that I had in suetes of lawe, but I thrived resonable well, yet I loste moch."

There is no reference to the Spanish Armada in 1588; but "the 30. of Jun A. Y. and I fell out," and "this yere I began to practise necromancy and to calle aungells and spirits." The following year was "wonderfull troblesome," and in spite of his continued practising of "nigromancy and magik and phisick" the diarist writes "my enimise prevailed againste me."

The third alchemical entry occurs on 17th June 1590, about five years after the first: "I distilled my strong water for the stone." However, the work was not taken very far, owing to other pressing claims. In July, Forman was called to appear before the Star Chamber; in October he sickened; in November he was hurt in the face; and to add to his preoccupations he "was offred a wife mani tymes this yere . . . and had the sight and choise of 4 or 5 maids and wydowes."

These distractions from alchemy and other professional pursuits continued, for in 1592 he "went first a woing to An Nok," and in 1593 he "went first a woing to Mrs. Lodcaster." The results are not stated; but by the end of 1593 alchemical prospects were improving, for the year's record ends: "This yere I stilled my strong water, for the which I gote moch mony."

The year 1594 opened badly, for "the 10. of Januari, at 30. past 5 p.m. I fell downe the staires." This entry follows in a suspicious sequence the last one quoted. Although troubled often by "the discourtasi of A. All.," Forman turned once more to his profitable alchemical exercises: "This yere I distilled moch strong water, and divers other waters, and made many sirupes. I gote moch money and paid all my old dettes almoste. Abought Michelmas I first begane to practise the philosopher's stone." At this point, although he had newly written a book of magic, and that on virgin parchment, ill-luck once more dogged the magician. "This yere Mrs. Broddedy thought I wold have maried her, but I entended yt not, and she disliked me moch till St. Jean's tyd. The 9. of Decemb. I fell downe the stairs again at 5 p.m." Mrs. B. had evidently been handed the attracting philtre in mistake for the repelling one; and Simon seems to have confused Saturn losing his feathers for the ascensive sign of the white swan.[1]

Simon Forman, whatever his failings, did not lack persistence. He picked himself up, and in Lent of 1595 "began the philosopher's stone" once more; also he made "many sirups and drugs, and distilled many waters, and bought stills." Unfortunately, however, "the 2. of May a jar fell out betwen A. Al. and myself ... for that Jone lefte hir apron at my house, and she was syck about yt." That Simon's interest in the stone was still alive on 26th September is shown in the entry for that day: "At 10 a.m. I went to Av. All, and we conferred with her, and she wold not be frendes to me, and we departed in yre. This dai p.m. at 55 past 3 I bought a peyer of newe black stockins, cost 12s., and that morning I drempt of 3 black rats, and of my philosophical pouder which I was distilling of." The unhappy sequel—portended no doubt by the 3 black rats, and not to be averted even by the master of sprites—came in the following December: "The 12. dai of Decemb. was a wonderfull unlucky dai to me. I brast 2 glasses and lest the water, and many things framed evill in my handes, and I was very unfortunat that dai, especially from 10 of the clock till night."

Another black sequence followed in 1596: "The 5. of March, Friday, I put on my newe furd gowne, a.m. 6. The 9. March I put on my velvet jerkin, a.m. at 9. The 12. March, Friday, p.m. 30 past 5, I went to garden, wher I found A. Al., and we becam frendes againe. The 29. March A. Al. hit me in the mouth with her hand. The 5. of Aprill, Monday, A. Al. scratched me by the face that I bled. ... The 27. of Aprill in subliming, my pot and glasse brok, and all my labour was lost pro lapide."

This is the last reference to the stone, and to alchemy in general, except for a mention of the preparation in the

[1] Ref. 11, p. 204

following year of syrups, distilled waters, and drugs. Forman married at last, in 1599, his bride being " An Baker of Kent, Sir Edward Monninges sisters daughter," a girl of sixteen. His improved circumstances are illustrated by an entry in 1600 : " This sommer I had my own pictur drawen, and mad my purple gowne, my velvet cap, my velvet cote, my velvet breches, my taffety cloke, my hat, and many other thinges, and did let my hear and berd growe."[1] Our alchemist was now at the height of his prosperity and fame, and despite the continued presence of flies in the ointment (" the 23. of Novembr. my wif and I fell out for her folly and negligence ") we may leave him living in dignity and comfort, as he reflects at the end of 1601, in the last few lines of his diary : " This yere I thrived, thankes be to God, resonable well."

[1] From these particulars it appears that the engraving reproduced in Plate 13 may have been derived from the portrait made in the summer of 1600, when Forman was forty-seven.

Chapter Three

THE ALCHEMIST IN ART

Introductory

EMBLEMS of alchemy entered at many points into the marvellous art of the Middle Ages; for alchemical symbolism often found an expression in decorative architecture, in stone, and in coloured glass. Alchemy was indissolubly linked with medieval art.

"For the thought written in stone," says Victor Hugo, "there existed at that period a privilege perfectly comparable to the present liberty of the press. It was the liberty of architecture." This liberty was occasionally used to record alchemical ideas. As an example, some of the decorative sculpture of Notre-Dame, which at one time was a resort of Hermetic philosophers, carried an alchemical significance.

Nicolas Flamel, also in Paris, blended the art of the architect and sculptor with that of the painter, in the famous alchemical frescoes with which he adorned the churchyard of the Innocents, at the beginning of the fifteenth century. Similarly, in London, Ripley's allusion to "*Westminster* Church, To whych these *Phylosophers* do haunte," calls to mind Ashmole's reference to a stained glass window in St. Margaret's Church, with a design symbolizing the processes of the Great Work, and his further mention of an alchemical painting which formerly adorned an arched wall in Westminster Abbey. The repeated occurrence of alchemical designs in ecclesiastical precincts is suggestive of the close parallel which the mystical alchemists were wont to draw between the Christian mystery of the spiritual Trinity and the alchemical mystery of the philosopher's stone, a material trinity in unity.

Plate 14   Melencolia (*page 57*)
(Dürer)

Plate 15   An Alchemist at Work *(page 63)*
(Brueghel)

Such forms of art as these were used in order to express abstract alchemical conceptions rather than humanistic alchemy. It is to the art of the painter and engraver that we must now turn for light upon the personality, environment, and methods of work of the alchemist. To such manifestations of art, historical chemistry owes a great debt which is seldom recognized.

Dürer's "Melencolia"

Early in the sixteenth century the famous German artists and engravers, Albrecht Dürer and Lucas Cranach, were influenced to some extent by alchemical ideas and symbolism, but they left no pictorial impression of an alchemist or his laboratory. Dürer (1471–1528), one of the two greatest artists Germany has ever produced, was particularly skilled in drawing on the block for the wood-cutter and in engraving on copper with his own unsurpassed hand. In 1513 and 1514 he wrought three engravings on copper that will rank for all time among the world's select masterpieces of this form of art: these were "The Knight" (1513), "St. Jerome in his Study" (1514), and "Melencolia" (1514).

There is no evidence that Dürer had an acquaintance with alchemy so intimate as that of Chaucer in an earlier age (page 29); nevertheless, alchemy formed an essential ingredient of the cultural background of his times. To contemporary men of culture in general, as to the alchemist in particular, the "Melencolia" (Plate 14) must have appeared as a rich repository of the pictorial symbolism of alchemy.

The numeral "I" following the engraved title suggests at once that Dürer had it in mind to design and execute a series of four copper-engravings illustrating the four temperaments: melancholic, phlegmatic, choleric, and sanguine. These were linked in the medieval mind with certain other mystical groups of 4, a magical number inherited from the early civilizations which flourished long before the time of Pythagoras.

The four temperaments were connected immediately with the four humours of the body (black bile, phlegm, yellow bile, blood); somewhat more remotely with the four outstanding colours of alchemy (black, white, citrine, red); and eventually with the four elements (earth, water, air, fire). The number 4 is emphasized in the magic square [1] shown so prominently in Dürer's design. The rainbow, seen in the background, was the alchemist's favourite symbol for the colours that were held to appear, in a definite sequence culminating in red, in the Vase of Hermes, during the operations of the Great Work, or preparation of the philosopher's stone. The magic square, the compasses, the polyhedron and sphere, are all symbolical of the Pythagorean insistence on the importance of number and form in the Cosmos. The Pythagorean and Platonic conceptions formed an important constituent of alchemical doctrine; further, the compasses, the balance, and the hour-glass, with its graduated scale, are suggestive of a common alchemical dictum, borrowed from *The Wisdom of Solomon*: "Thou hast ordered all things in measure and number and weight."

The alchemical significance of the crucible requires no explanation; for this most familiar of all pieces of alchemical apparatus was to be found in every alchemist's laboratory, den, or kitchen. The most familiar agent used by the alchemists in their operations was fire; so much so, that the alchemist was often called "the child of fire." Fire was commonly symbolized by cutting, penetrating, or wounding implements and tools, like the saw and plane and the hammer and nails of Dürer's design. The alchemical imagination bodied forth fire in another form as sophic sulphur, one of the two final ingredients of the philosopher's stone, and occasionally shown in the similitude of a dog. The second

[1] The magic square of the 4th order (*i.e.*, containing the consecutive numbers 1 to 4^2 and adding up in various directions to a constant sum) shows the date of the engraving (1514) in the two middle cells of the bottom row. Similar magic squares of the orders 3 to 9 were constructed by Dürer's contemporary, Cornelius Agrippa, and assigned to Saturn, Jupiter, Mars, Sol, Venus, Mercury, and Luna. Such squares were sometimes engraved on plates of the corresponding metals and worn as amulets.

ingredient, sophic mercury, was sometimes represented by water; that is to say, "our water" of the Hermetic Stream, or "heavy water," not wetting the hands. Alternatively, this "philosophical water" was regarded as a menstruum uniting sophic sulphur and sophic mercury. Occasionally the seeker after the stone is shown balancing the opposed elements, fire and water, in a pair of scales, and at one time it was imagined that, in alcohol, such a combination of irreconcilables had been achieved.

The seven-runged ladder is another common feature of alchemical symbolism, the rungs representing the seven metals and the associated heavenly bodies. One of the paintings of *Splendor Solis* (1582), for example, shows a man standing on the sixth and seventh rungs (representing silver and gold) and gathering the golden fruit of the Philosophic Tree, from the roots of which issues the Hermetic Stream. In the later *Mutus Liber* a young man, using a stone for his pillow, is shown asleep at the foot of a ladder bearing ascending and descending angels; this stone, upon which Jacob poured oil, was sometimes accepted as a symbol of the philosopher's stone.

We may come now to the central theme of Dürer's "Melencolia." The alchemist's lot was such that he was often depicted as a melancholy and frustrated being, as, for example, by Chaucer, Weiditz, Brueghel, and Teniers. In a wider sense, melancholy was held to be an attribute of students, or seekers after knowledge. The doctrine of melancholy, moreover, is inseparable from the Saturn mysticism which permeates alchemy. This association, which was widely recognized in the early sixteenth century, finds many reflections in Dürer's masterpiece. One of the elements of Saturnine mysticism is measurement, typified by the compasses, balance, and hour-glass. The polyhedron lying beside the foot of the ladder (representing the base metal, lead) may be an image of the philosopher's stone, or, more immediately, of that so-called "Stone of Saturn," which Kronos, or Saturn, "swallowed and spewed up instead of Jupiter." As already mentioned (p. 11), Saturn, who is often represented in alchemy as an old man with an hour-glass upon his head, was addicted to swallowing his own children; for this reason, infants, usually shown at play, enter into the Saturnine elements of alchemy.

It is frequently stated in the esoteric writings on alchemy that once the primitive materials of the stone have been obtained, the rest of the operations of the Great Work are " only a labour fit for women, or child's play." [1] This *ludus puerorum* motive often comes to the surface in sixteenth-century art,[2] as, for example, in the work of Dürer's contemporary, Cranach. The infants may be linked on the one hand with the alchemical idea of regeneration, and on the other with the mythological story of Saturn, and thus with the conception of melancholy.

All three of Cranach's representations of Melancholy show infants at play. In the first (1528), four infants are romping with a dog, a sphere and compasses being shown in the background; in the second (1532), two of three infants are trying to lever forward a large sphere, the third has a hoop, and there is a dog in the background; in the third (1533), fifteen infant boys are shown at play, of whom some are dancing and two are playing on the flute and drum. There are other examples in alchemy suggesting the use of music as an antidote to melancholy (p. 70).

One of the paintings of *Splendor Solis* (1582) shows ten infant boys at play, and the accompanying bath provides still another link with the Saturn mysticism, which was often associated with moisture or wetness. Thus Saturn, in the guise of a crippled or wooden-legged man[3] with a watering-pot, is sometimes shown watering the sun-tree and moon-tree of the alchemists. Again, the " labour fit for women " is frequently brought out in alchemical pictures of washerwomen engaged in their humid operations. From this point

---

[1] Ref. 11, pp. 134, 238, 267

[2] For a discussion of some alchemical themes in Renaissance art see G. F. Hartlaub's " Arcana Artis," in *Zeitschrift für Kunstgeschichte*, 1938, 6, p. 289

[3] Symbolizing the slow and melancholy planet, Saturn, and the dull and heavy metal, lead, with which the planet was associated in alchemy

of view it is interesting that Dürer's design has a watery background.

The sphere and hoop associated with Cranach's infants are suggestive also of change and regeneration. They may perhaps be linked with that still older symbol of ancient Egypt, the serpent biting its own tail, signifying eternity. Other alchemical conceptions closely bound up with the sphere and hoop, and the grindstone upon which Dürer's infant is sitting, are those of the philosopher's egg, or Vase of Hermes, and the circulation within it of the materials of the Great Work. The bulging purse at the foot of Dürer's main figure may also be likened to the purse into which one of three winged infants is dropping coins, in a celebrated alchemical interior of Teniers (p. 78); in the same painting a large soap-bubble hovering in the air is reminiscent of the sphere in the compositions of Dürer and Cranach. The rolling sphere, hoop, or grindstone may also be connected with the famous second precept of Hermes: "What is below is like that which is above, and what is above is like that which is below, to accomplish the miracles of one thing."

Dürer's brooding figure, posed in an attitude of dejection and frustration, "with a sad leaden downward cast," may be interpreted as an embodiment of the alchemical searcher after the stone—or, in a wider sense, as the seeker after wisdom—in a mood of temporary defeat:

> Low-seated she leans forward massively,
>   With cheek on clenched left hand, the forearm's might
> Erect, its elbow on her rounded knee;
>   Across a clasped book in her lap the right
> Upholds a pair of compasses; she gazes
> With full set eyes, but wandering in thick mazes
>   Of sombre thought beholds no outward sight.[1]

The atmosphere of lassitude and gloom is intensified by the tolling bell, the quiescent infant, and the lean and passive hound. Despite the opening keys and the light-giving lamp,

[1] James Thomson, ref. 16

"knowledge comes, but wisdom lingers." Yet, "we fall to rise, are baffled to fight better." In the distance, dispelling the "black bat, night," shines the sun over the Saturnine sea; and if, like the Saturnine symbols of alchemy, the winged genius of Melencolia broods with darkened face, Milton tells us why:

> Hail! divinest Melancholy!
> Whose saintly visage is too bright
> To hit the sense of human sight,
> And therefore to our weaker view
> O'erlaid with black, staid Wisdom's hue.

Weiditz

One of the earliest surviving representations of a medieval alchemist at work is a woodcut by Hans Weiditz, a contemporary of Dürer and Cranach. Weiditz was an outstanding illustrator of the Augsburg school; he is often called the "Petrarcameister," because of the rich array of woodcuts with which he illustrated the German translation of Petrarch's *De Remediis*—the so-called *Trostspiegel*, published in 1532. His historical woodcut of an alchemist at work (Plate 8) first appeared in this book, although it was executed about 1520; like so many other early engravings, it was used in later books without mention of the original source.

Weiditz's alchemist is certainly melancholy of mien. His laboratory may be described as a blacksmith's forge besprinkled with crucibles and primitive glass vessels. The most complex device is a simple still; the spare alembic, helm, or still-head, lying on the bench, suggests that this unit—with its long and vulnerable beak—was the weak part of the apparatus.

The decline of German painting at the end of the sixteenth century was followed by the remarkable rise and development of the Flemish and Dutch schools. It is to the paintings of the Flemish and Dutch masters that we are chiefly indebted for pictorial impressions of alchemists and alchemical interiors, although subjects of this kind were also rendered to a less extent in Italy, Spain, Germany, and other countries.

Brueghel

Among the early masters[1] of the Flemish and Dutch schools, and one of the greatest of them all, was Pieter Brueghel the Elder (1525–69), born at Breughel near Breda. In the iconography of alchemy, Brueghel occupies an important position on account of his remarkable picture of an alchemist at work (1558), which has become widely known through the engraving of it made by the Flemish artist and publisher, Hieronimus Cock (1510–70). This engraving, like so much of Cock's work, was originally somewhat slight and thin, and later prints from the plate retouched by Theodore Galle show no improvement (Plate 15). In any state this engraving is very rare: it measures about $17\frac{1}{2}$ by 12 inches, and reproduces the original painting in reverse.

Brueghel's treatment of the subject is piquant and distinctive. The alchemist, a curious figure, disreputable and untidy, is working *en famille*, and yet aloof, in a room which evidently serves the dual purpose of laboratory and kitchen. He is heating a crucible and a couple of pots, and at the same time dropping his last coin into another crucible. The raw materials required for the activities of the kitchen seem to have been replaced by those used in the operations of transmutation, and even the kitchen utensils have been pressed into the same all-absorbing service. The dominant notes are untidiness and poverty. A paper pinned up above the alchemist at his working bench bears prominently the word "misero." The neglected wife attempts in vain to shake another coin out of the empty purse, whilst her lord and master, oblivious to the wants of his family, makes his final sacrifice on the altar of Hermes. The children ransack the empty store-cupboard in an unrewarded search for scraps of food; one of them wears an empty pot inverted over his head.

[1] For details of these and other painters and engravers see ref. 1

An apathetic laborant is working a pair of bellows—judging from his facial expression, under protest. The only figure showing any sign of enthusiasm is that of a robed acolyte who appears to be declaiming, for his own satisfaction, a passage from an alchemical tome lying open on a desk before him. The inset picture, appearing as if viewed through a window, shows the next act in the drama: the alchemist and his wife, with their three children—one of them, with child-like persistence, still wearing his novel headgear—are being received into the poorhouse.

A satirical French verse attached to the engraving invites the beholder to gaze upon this dolt, who in his fruitless quest distils away his goods, his senses, and his children's bread. There is a Dutch verse to the same general effect. The more prominent Latin subscription, written in Leonine hexameters of indifferent quantity, indicates that the material of the stone and the four elements abound everywhere but can be discerned only by the initiated. Thus the verses, like the picture, constitute a satire directed against the arbitrary operations of the puffer.

In his work *De Natura Rerum* (Concerning the Nature of Things), Paracelsus contrasts the spagyric (alchemistic) physicians of that day with the "lazy, so-called" physicians who prefer dogma to experiment, and prepare their medicines without recourse to alchemy and fire:

For they are not given to idleness, nor go in a proud habit, or plush and velvet garments, often showing their rings upon their fingers, or wearing silver daggers by their side, or fine and gay gloves upon their hands; but they diligently follow their labours, sweating whole days and nights by their fiery furnaces. They do not go out promenading, but take delight in their laboratory. They wear leathern garments with a pouch, and an apron upon which to wipe their hands. They put their fingers amongst the coals, the lute, and the dung, not into golden rings. They are sooty and black like smiths and colliers, and do not pride themselves upon a sleek countenance. They do not gossip with their patients and vaunt their own remedies. They know well that the work must glorify the workman, not the workman his

Plate 16 PVLVIS PYRIVS (page 67)
(Stradanus)

Plate 17 The Oratory and the Laboratory (*page 69*)
(Vriese)

work. They reject such vanities, and delight to labour in the fire and learn the steps of alchemy. These are distillation, solution, putrefaction, extraction, calcination, reverberation, sublimation, fixation, separation, reduction, coagulation, tincture, and the like.

The notes of caricature and satire are lacking, so far as the laboratory workers are concerned, but otherwise this literary description conforms in broad outline to the artistic delineations of alchemists given by Weiditz and Brueghel in their drawings of the same period.

Brueghel's picture is particularly valuable for the information it gives about the equipment of a laboratory of his time; for the composition is evidently based upon observations made by the artist himself. Crucibles are still the commonest pieces of apparatus; pots and pans are plentiful; and there are also tubs, jugs, glass flasks, pestles and mortars, stills, filters, a sieve, a basket of charcoal, some primitive drug-jars, hand-bellows, tongs, trowel, and a furnace for boiling water. The hour-glass and scales point to incipient measurement and quantitative work.

According to Paracelsus, in equipping an alchemical laboratory, "there is need of nothing else but a foundry, bellows, tongs, hammers, cauldrons, jars, and cupels made from beechen ashes"; but in another place he adds to these, "glass vessels, cucurbites, circulators, vessels of Hermes, earthen vessels, baths, blast-furnaces, reverbatories, and instruments of like kind, also marble, coals, and tongs."

There is another painting by Pieter Brueghel the Elder, entitled "De Magere Keucken" (The Scanty Kitchen). This is a droll, almost grotesque, study of a poverty-stricken kitchen crammed with lean and hungry figures, comic relief being afforded by a very portly visitor. The cook, bending with a lean and hungry look over a pot on the hearth, bears a close resemblance in general appearance, attire, and pose to the alchemist; a small child has its head immersed in an empty pot, as in the alchemical scene.

Pieter Brueghel the Elder was an artist of surpassing genius and originality. Many of his drawings and paintings were concerned with Bible subjects, proverbial sayings, and medieval ideas of heaven, earth, hell, the devil, and death. He was fond of depicting peasant life, village scenes, and odd characters, and he took a particular delight in the bizarre. He was a consummate master of landscape painting. His personality and interests earned for him the familiar name of "Boeren Brueghel," or "Farmer Brueghel." His sons, Pieter and Jan, were also painters of distinction. Pieter Brueghel the Younger (1564–1638) was known as "Höllen [Hell] Brueghel," because of the macabre nature of his subjects; his son, Pieter, was also an artist. Jan Brueghel (1568–1625) affected velvet attire, and was often called "Fluweelen [Velvet] Brueghel"; his landscape paintings included some interesting and elegant allegorical representations of the four elements, which he treated in pairs for this purpose. His son, also called Jan, was an artist; his daughter, Anna, married David Teniers the younger.

Stradanus

Jan van der Straet, or Johannes Stradanus (1523–1605), a Flemish contemporary of the elder Brueghel, gave a very different impression of an alchemical interior, in a painting that was engraved [1] by Philip Galle and entitled "Distillatio." The dominant process it represents is distillation. Many stills are figured in full operation, and four laborants are busily engaged with them. Another laborant works a screw-press with a long wooden lever, and a laboratory boy operates a pestle hanging from a springy wooden lath. Two other figures are actively engaged at furnaces in the background. The director of the laboratory, wearing a doctor's cap, sits in a comfortable armchair and refers to an open book in consultation with a colleague standing behind him. On the floor lies a sheaf of grain, typifying the vital principle. The dominant note of the picture is ordered and affluent activity, in contrast to the disorder and

---

[1] The engraving is reproduced in F. Ferchl and A. Süssenguth's *Kurzgeschichte der Chemie*, Mittenwald, 1936

poverty of Brueghel's picture. An inset panel even shows the director and his wife partaking of an enjoyable meal at the end of the day's work. This composition has little in common with the Flemish and Dutch treatments of the subject. The painting depicts such a laboratory as Trismosin is said to have worked in at Ponteleone, near Venice, about 1476. "I never saw such laboratory work, in all kinds of Particular Processes and medicines, as in that place," wrote Trismosin.

Stradanus's picture probably represents an Italian laboratory of the second half of the sixteenth century. The painter worked a good deal in Italy, and died at Florence in 1605. A fresco [1] in the same style by Stradanus, dated 1570, depicts some of the same workers engaged in similar operations. Another of his paintings, entitled "Pulvis Pyrius" (Gunpowder), was engraved about the year 1570, also by the Dutchman, Philip Galle (1537–1612), whose son Theodore Galle (1571–1633) had a hand in the engraving of the elder Brueghel's alchemical painting. Like painting in the Brueghel family, engraving was a hereditary talent in the Galle family for several generations.

The elder Galle's engraving of "Pulvis Pyrius" (Plate 16) measures 26·5 by 19 cm. The subject of this picture is the interior of a cannon foundry, probably Italian, in which skilled workmen are carrying out various operations in the casting and finishing of large guns. On the left, a man within a tread-wheel supplies the power for working a lathe. On the right, there is a panel depicting the bombardment and destruction of a fort by a battery of this early artillery. At the back, an inset shows Berthold Schwarz in his laboratory, making the crucial discovery of the propellent force of gunpowder. A Latin inscription at the foot of the engraving hits off the medieval attitude towards the ultimate origin of gunpowder by stating "That thunders and thunderbolts should be brandished in the hand was surely a gift from the envious powers below."

Stradanus's animated paintings deal with the activities

[1] Reproduced in E. J. Holmyard's *Makers of Chemistry*, Oxford, 1931

of skilled laborants and workmen, who are shown tackling their clearly defined tasks with energy and zest. The artist reflects the severely practical outlook of craftsmen of that era, Biringuccio, Agricola, and Benvenuto Cellini, for example. He delineates the man of action, not the man of dreams who takes the centre of the stage in the typical alchemical compositions of the Flemish and Dutch painters.

DE BRY

The de Brys, who migrated from Liège to Frankfurt-on-Main, were another family of engravers by heredity, whose first two members, Theodorus (*b.* 1528) and Johannes Theodorus (*b.* 1561), were contemporaries of Philip and Theodore Galle, respectively. Many artistic copper engravings of great interest in their alchemical symbolism were executed by Johannes Theodorus de Bry in particular, notably the emblems in Count Michael Maier's *Atalanta Fugiens*, which first appeared in 1617 or 1618.[1]

One of these emblems[2] depicts an alchemist labouring in the fire; but, unlike the drawings of Weiditz, Brueghel, and Stradanus, this engraving is purely formal and devoid of any realistic detail. After the death of the younger de Bry in 1623 his engraving, printselling, and publishing business was continued at Frankfurt by his two sons-in-law, Matthew Merian and William Fitzer, and the engraving tradition persisted in the Merian family for two more generations, until the eighteenth century. It is interesting that William Fitzer, who married de Bry's youngest daughter in 1625, was a Londoner who settled in Frankfurt and later in Heidelberg.

THE MYSTICAL ALCHEMIST IN ART

Alchemists have often been divided into two classes, denoted by such names as alchemists and pseudo-alchemists,

[1] For an artistic and technical evaluation of these and other alchemical engravings, with cognate bibliographical details, see ref. 15

[2] Reproduced in ref. 12

Plate 18   David Teniers (*page 73*)
(Self-portrait)

Plate 19 Le Chimiste (*page 75*)
(Teniers)

esoteric alchemists and exoteric alchemists, adepts and puffers, hermetics and charlatans, and such like. This simple classification is both arbitrary and inadequate. As already stated (p. 23), the spectrum of alchemical thought and action showed all the colours of the rainbow, or the peacock's tail, extending from the infra-red to the ultra-violet. Or, to change the metaphor, alchemy was not a two-party system: in the *Turba philosophorum*, or parliament of alchemy, there were all shades of opinion and conduct, ranging from the extreme left to the extreme right. Alchemy could degenerate into the depths of hocus-pocus and fraud, or it could reach sublime heights under the stimulus and inspiration of philosophy and religion. Between the charlatans and puffers on the one extreme and the philosophers and religious mystics on the other, stood the solid alchemical party of the centre: that body of devoted craftsmen who sustained and developed a practical tradition upon which modern chemistry was destined to be based. In the realm of art, Ben Jonson depicted the charlatan, Brueghel the puffer, Stradanus the middle-man, and de Bry the mystic. But no matter what the type, any realistic presentation of the alchemist, whether in literature or in art, must of necessity focus upon the all-absorbing nature of his pursuit, his intense abstraction, his forgetfulness of time and place, and the concentration of all the powers of his being upon one objective, after the manner of Balthazar Claes, in Balzac's masterpiece (p. 28).

The extreme type of the spiritual alchemist, or religious mystic, is illustrated in a curious drawing of an alchemist in his laboratory, which appeared in Khunrath's *Amphitheatrum Sapientiae Æternae*, published at Hanau in 1609.[1] Heinrich Khunrath, occultist, theosophist and cabbalist, was a Hermetic mystic of the most pronounced type, who has been claimed as "a hierophant of the psychic side of the *magnum opus*." This drawing (Plate 17) was executed after Khunrath's own design, apparently by a member of the

[1] This 1609 edition was posthumous. The extremely rare first edition of 1595 (possibly published at Hamburg) seems to have been issued privately to certain adepts.

THE ALCHEMIST IN ART

de Vries family. The rendering is formal, and in some respects almost diagrammatic; the perspective effect is reminiscent of some of the work of Jan de Vries (b. 1527) and also of J. T. de Bry.[1] The numerous inscriptions are partly explanatory but mostly mystical. The tabernacle on the left is designated as the oratorium, or oratory; facing it, on the right, is the laboratorium, or laboratory. The tabernacle bears the Name of the Lord in Hebrew characters, and on its left fold is a Latin inscription, *Hoc hoc agentibus nobis, aderit ipse Deus* (When we attend strictly to our work, God himself will help us).

The kneeling alchemist is Khunrath himself. As he prays, his eyes rest upon a pentagram, the badge of the Pythagoreans. Perhaps he is praying in the spirit of George Ripley, canon of Bridlington in the foregoing century: " O Unity in the substance, and Trinity in the Godhead. . . . As thou didst make all things out of *one* chaos, so let me be skilled to evolve our microcosm [the philosopher's stone] out of *one* substance in its three aspects of Magnesia, Sulphur, and Mercury." The importance attached to music, harmony, number, and proportion in the operations of the Great Work, already suggested by the symbol of the pentagram, is emphasized by the musical instruments and pair of scales lying on the central table; moreover, the attached Latin inscription indicates that sacred music disperses sadness (or alchemic melancholia) and evil spirits. A stellate lamp with seven points, from each of which issues a small flame, hangs from the ceiling.

The laboratory is adorned with the inscriptions: *Nec temere, nec timide* (Neither rashly nor timidly), and *Sapienter retentatum, succedet aliquando* (That which is wisely tried again will succeed sometime). The two outer pillars of the canopy over the alchemical hearth have a symbolical as well as a material significance, for they bear the words *Ratio* (Reason) and *Experientia* (Experience). Even the small still and athanor shown in the foreground are provided with mystic inscriptions. The athanor, containing the sealed Vessel of Hermes, which may have to " stand in the fyre " for at least a philosopher's month (p. 15), is significantly labelled *Festina lente* (Hasten

[1] See e.g. Plate 6

gently). Over the doorway at the far end are inscribed the words *Dormiens vigila* (While sleeping, watch). A set of "reagent bottles" arranged above the canopy of this rarefied laboratory carry such apposite "labels" as: *Hyle* (matter), *Ros celi* (dew of the sky), ☉ *potab.* (potable gold), *Azoth* (sophic mercury), and *Sang.* with a serpentine symbol (dragon's blood).

In spirit, although not in material or design, Khunrath's oratory-laboratory is akin to the alchemist's cell which Bishop Hugh of Besançon constructed, according to Victor Hugo, in one of the ancient towers of Notre-Dame de Paris early in the fourteenth century. Victor Hugo, depicting its appearance in the year 1482, describes it as "a sombre, dimly lighted cell," with dust and cobwebs covering its chaotic assortment of compasses, alembics, bottles, retorts, skeletons of animals, manuscripts, and all the flotsam and jetsam of the alchemical practitioner. Its walls were covered with legends in many tongues and characters, such as *Unde? Inde?* (Whence? Hence?); *Homo homini monstrum* (Man is a monster unto men); *Sapere aude* (Dare to be wise); and rhyming jingles like *Nomen numen* (The name, a wonder), and *Astra castra* (The stars, a fortune)—"the whole crossed and recrossed in all directions with stars and triangles, human and animal figures, till the wall of the cell looked like a sheet of paper over which a monkey has dragged a pen full of ink."[1] Even the bellows bore the words *Spiro spero* (Blow, hope), a favourite slogan of the alchemical fraternity which must have been of enduring service to the puffer.

At certain points on its vast front, alchemy impinged upon astrology and magic, and it is therefore not surprising that in art, as in literature, the astrologer and the magician have something in common with the alchemist. In literature, this relationship has been discussed above. In art, perhaps the most striking example of the kind is to be found in the celebrated etching of Doctor Faustus by Rembrandt van Rijn (1606–69), the most famous of the Dutch painters. Victor Hugo, who held it to be impossible to contemplate

[1] V. Hugo ref. 6

this masterpiece of " the Shakespeare of painting " without measureless admiration, describes it in vivid language :

There is a gloomy chamber ; in the middle stands a table loaded with mysterious and repulsive objects—death's heads, spheres, alembics, compasses, parchments covered with hieroglyphics. Behind this table, which hides the lower part of him, stands the Doctor wrapped in a wide gown, his head covered by a fur cap reaching to his eyebrows. He has partly risen from his immense arm-chair, his clenched fists are leaning on the table, while he gazes in curiosity and terror at a luminous circle of magic letters shining on the wall in the background like the solar spectrum in a camera obscura. This cabbalistic sun seems actually to scintillate, and fills the dim cell with its mysterious radiance. It is terrible and yet beautiful.

In this etching [1] Rembrandt probably made his closest approach to an alchemical subject. The Faust legend has inspired many other artists, among them Adriaen Jacobsz Matham, born at the Hague about 1600. His allegorical painting showing an alchemist in his study-laboratory, with a female figure and a demon in the background, might also be interpreted as a representation of the scene in Faust in which the vision of Helena appears in a magic mirror. It is interesting that among the " reagents " depicted on a shelf in the background are *opium* and *sanguis draconis* (dragon's blood).

Teniers

The elder Brueghel and Stradanus were eminent harbingers of that marvellous efflorescence of Flemish and Dutch painters whose work brought so much lustre and colour and grace into the seventeenth century. Most of these artists, like their prototype, " Farmer " Brueghel, were imbued with a deep love of the home and of the village life of their own peasantry. They delighted to paint genre studies of these familiar scenes, and of odd characters and quaint settings. Their keen eye for the odd and droll probably explains why so many of them turned for inspiration to that strange being, the alchemist, and his still stranger environment. Among

[1] Reproduced in G. de Givry's *Witchcraft, Magic and Alchemy*, London, 1931

Plate 20 An Alchemist in his Laboratory (*page 76*)
(Teniers)

Plate 21 An Alchemical Interior (*page 77*)
(Teniers)

many famous artists of this age, it is easy to single out David Teniers the Younger as alchemy's artist *par excellence*. His lifetime covered all but the first ten and the last six years of the seventeenth century.

The members of the Teniers family offer another remarkable example of inherited artistic ability. There were four David Teniers in direct succession, all of whom were painters; the first was born in 1582 and the fourth died in 1771, so that between them they spanned almost two centuries. The father of David Teniers the Elder (*b.* 1582) was Julian Teniers (or Taisner), a mercer of Antwerp. His sons Julian and David both became painters, David studying under Rubens and also at Rome. David Teniers the Younger (1610–94) was born at Antwerp, and worked originally in the studio of his father, from whom he derived his inspiration and style. He may have worked in Rubens' studio also, and in 1637 he married Anna Brueghel, at that time a pupil of Rubens. A younger brother, Abraham Teniers, was also a painter of note.

David Teniers the Younger (Plate 18) painted hundreds of pictures, embracing a great variety of subjects. He is distinguished by his light and spiritual touch, the cool harmony and transparency of his colours, and his delicate rendering of the finest details. He was so versatile that " there was no manner of painting which he could not imitate perfectly in a manner to deceive the finest connoisseurs "; but his chief interests centred in peasant life and in characters and scenes with a flavour of piquancy or drollery. He painted peasants drinking, peasants making merry, peasants at dinner, peasants playing skittles, peasants before a fire, boors regaling, peasants dancing, a peasant smoking, village fêtes and weddings, Flemish landscapes, interiors of inns, of farmhouses and kitchens, an old woman peeling a pear and another cutting tobacco, the toper, the piper, the knife-grinder, the sausage-maker, and the village doctor. The alchemist and his mysterious operations fascinated him, and he painted a large variety of pictures dealing with this inexhaustible theme.

Teniers, like so many of his contemporaries, did not lose

interest in a subject when he had painted it once or twice. He had the faculty of returning time after time to the same theme, treating it from a slightly different angle each time. This feature of Teniers' work was an important factor in his prodigal creativeness. Examples of his paintings are fairly common in the large museums and galleries of art; but his alchemical paintings are known to modern chemists—if they are known at all—chiefly through reproductions in books and journals of some of the line engravings that have been made from the originals. There is a considerable variety of such alchemical engravings after Teniers and other artists, some of them being works of great merit by talented engravers. Even the best of them, however, suffer from the unavoidable defect of giving no suggestion of the colours of the original paintings. Fortunately, a few of these paintings have been reproduced in colour by modern processes.

Another disadvantage, not always realized, is that many of the engravings are executed in reverse. Some, indeed, may be seen in both right-handed and left-handed forms; incidentally, one form is sometimes scarcer and more valuable than the other! Reversed engravings may usually be identified by the recognition in them of left-handed operators. Thus, in Pierre Basan's engraving of Teniers' painting sometimes known as " Le Grimoire d'Hypocrate " (The Black Book of Hippocrates), the central figure is stirring with the left hand and holding the Black Book in the right hand, which is clearly unnatural in a normal right-handed subject. In Francesco del Pedro's later engraving of the same painting these relationships are reversed, the disposition being identical with that of the original painting.[1] A right-handed plate, drawn to match the original, gives a left-handed print, which is therefore easier to produce than its mirror-image. Possibly del Pedro worked from Basan's left-handed engraving and thus reverted in his prints to the original form of the painting; alternatively, he may have cut his plate from a reflection of the original picture in a mirror.

A representative alchemical interior after Teniers is

[1] Plate 21 below; see also ref. 11, Plate 29

shown in Plate 19, which is a reproduction of an engraving in reverse by Michon and Lorieux. This picture is markedly different from the earlier alchemical representations of Weiditz and Brueghel. The element of caricature is absent, the central figure having a spiritual touch. The atmosphere of the laboratory is calm and orderly. The composition is brought to a focus in the alchemist. He is the central figure, illuminated by a beam of light from the open window. He is not working *en famille*: there are no distractions. The laboratory is neither a blacksmith's forge nor a converted kitchen. It is certainly not an oratory. It is a room designed and equipped expressly for the prosecution of alchemy. There is no sign of mysticism in the form either of the apparatus of magic or of inscriptions on the walls. One looks in vain for the athanor (the mystical House of the Chick) or the sealed Hermetic Vase of the adepts. In brief, this picture of Teniers bears out the aphorism of Liebig: "Alchemy was never at any time anything different from chemistry."

The details are rendered with the clearness and precision so characteristic of Teniers. The crucible no longer reigns supreme among the apparatus; it remains prominent, but the still is now coming into its own. Teniers' alchemists kept their apparatus, and even their books, mainly upon the floor: many pieces in glass and earthenware are so disposed in this picture. The large charcoal-bin is a characteristic feature, and so are the skull and the small painting affixed to the walls and the fish suspended from the ceiling. The suspended fish is sometimes replaced in representations of alchemical interiors by a salamander, or a crocodile; Gerard Dou and other contemporary painters sometimes show a model of an angel similarly placed in their pictures of doctors' consulting-rooms. Working after dark must have been difficult in this laboratory, as artificial light was apparently limited to two candle-power, provided by the candles fixed above and at the side of the chimney opening.

An impression of depth is given by the figures in the background, and the cat chasing a mouse in the intervening space. These are typical elements in a Teniers alchemical interior, and so is the spectator looking through the high window in the back wall.

As is usual with Teniers, the dominant colour note of the original painting lies in rich shades of brown, ranging from light browns, through red-browns, to chocolate tints. The alchemist's robe and soft hat are dark blue, trimmed at the edges with brown fur; a leather bag and a key hang from his girdle, and he wears loose slippers.

The original painting, which measures about 21 by 16 inches, is signed by the artist and dated 1648. It has had a chequered history. Before the French Revolution it was in the collection of the Duc d'Orléans, together with other paintings by Teniers. Later, it remained for many years in private ownership in England. Since 1937 it has been in the Fisher collection of alchemical and historical pictures at Pittsburgh, Pennsylvania.

A more elaborate type of alchemical interior by Teniers is shown in a painting in the Dresden collection (Plate 20). This large laboratory has two hearths, each with a capacious chimney of masonry to carry off smoke and fumes. The hearth in the background has an open fire which is kept alive with the help of a large pair of bellows, as in a blacksmith's forge. The smaller enclosed fires on the other hearth, in the foreground, are kept going with hand-bellows. The apparatus on this hearth is arranged in a very neat and workmanlike way: the alchemist is able to keep his crucible at the right heat and at the same time to watch a distillation from a still fitted with a two-beaked alembic. The still on the floor in the foreground, with independent firing and a water-cooled helm, is a common piece of apparatus in Teniers' laboratories; it was sometimes called the "Moor's head," owing to a fancied resemblance between the shape of the cooling jacket and a Moorish turban.

Among the smaller accessories, the hour-glass, portable candlestick, and dried poppy-heads appeal to the eye and to the imagination. The active cat of the smaller laboratory

Plate 22   Alchemical Cupids (*page 78*)
(Teniers)

Plate 23 The Alchemist (*page 80*)
(Steen)

Plate 24 L'Alchymiste en Méditation (*page 82*)
(Wijck)

Plate 25 Le Ménage du Chimiste *(page 83)*
(Wijck)

has been replaced by a quiescent dog, which watches the mouse with little more than formal interest. The familiar group in the background again lends an appearance of depth to the room; the central figure of this group, holding a small flask, appears to be a portrait of Teniers himself. Apart from the broken alembic lying on the floor, everything is neatly arranged; in general, the laboratory creates an impression of efficiency and purposefulness.

In this composition Teniers makes free and effective use of various shades of brown; bluish-grey tones are also prominent. The suspended fish is dull green; the glowing points of the fires, as usual, are bright red.[1]

Some appreciation of Teniers' many variations on the alchemical theme may be gained by comparing the last-named painting (Plate 20) with "Le Grimoire d'Hypocrate" (Plate 21). In the original paintings the chief figure is placed in the left foreground, facing left. There is little difference in the backgrounds of the two compositions, the main window, bellows, hearth, group of figures, and suspended fish being common features. In "Le Grimoire" the small back window with the spectator is omitted, while in the foreground the round table has been moved to the left, replacing the hearth of the other picture. Moreover, instead of the "Moor's head" there is a charcoal-bin, and a grindstone has been substituted for the anvil in the background.

Alchemical paintings, like others, have often been copied, sometimes with great faithfulness by pupils or admirers of the original painters.[2] Occasionally these copies are wrongly

[1] A handsome nineteenth-century reproduction of this painting was issued as a Hanfstaengl print (in black and white and also in colour), from an engraving by C. Straub. See Plate 20.

[2] There is, for example, such a faithful copy in the St. Andrews collection, made by J. J. Rink in 1793. In 1755, the original, then "In the Collection of Hen: Isaac Esqr.," was engraved in reverse by T. Major, under the title of "The 'Laboratory," (*i.e.* The Elaboratory), and inscribed to William Pitcairn M.D. An unreversed engraving of the same painting, by Jorma, was published in Paris with the title, "Le Jeune Chimiste." For a reproduction in colour of Rink's painting see the frontispiece of the present work, also *Endeavour*, 1945, 4, p. 94.

regarded as originals. In some instances the copyist has endeavoured to improve upon the original. For example, an attractive painting of "Le Grimoire," formerly in the collection of Sir William Pope,[1] shows an extra figure of a boy standing in the middle, where the original composition (Plate 21) showed only empty space. Some fresh apparatus has been put on the floor in the foreground, and a vessel and a sketch hang on the wall above the alchemist's head. This painting was attributed to "T. Wyck," although it is a typical Teniers composition, with none of Wyck's outstanding characteristics.

Teniers also rings the changes upon the alchemist himself. He is usually shown as an elderly and sedate man; sometimes, however, he is younger; or he may be a hunchback, or even an ape. Teniers' famous caricature of the lowest kind of puffer, apeing unintelligently the operations of the thinking and informed alchemist, shows an ape seated at the hearth and manipulating the bellows: it bears the satirical title, "Le Plaisir des Fous" (The Amusement of Fools).[2] Another composition, in complete contrast, depicts three cupids as sole tenants of the laboratory. Two of these, representing the alchemist and his famulus, are busy at the hearth, while the other is putting coins into a purse lying on the familiar round table with the ornamented tripartite foot (Plate 22). A large iridescent soap-bubble hovers in the air, in the place usually occupied by the suspended fish. This charming composition is presumably based upon the *ludus puerorum* motive in alchemy, and since the purse is being filled, instead of emptied, it appears that the Great Work is indeed "child's play" to these alchemical cupids.

Teniers, unlike Brueghel, Steen, and van Ostade, does not introduce neglected wives, with purses empty and quivers full, to impede the practical work going on in his laboratories. It is true that engravings after Teniers, bearing alchemical titles, sometimes show a woman in the room,

---

[1] Professor of Chemistry in the University of Cambridge, 1908–1939

[2] A reproduction of an engraving by Basan of this painting appeared in *Endeavour*, 1945, 4, p. 95

but this is due to the engraver exercising a kind of engraver's licence with the title. There is, for example, an engraving after Teniers by J. P. Le Bas, entitled " Le Chymiste." At first sight, the central figure, gazing intently at a liquid in a small round-bottomed flask which he holds in one hand, appears to be an alchemist. As a matter of fact, however, he is a doctor seated at a table in his consulting-room, examining a specimen of urine in a vessel formerly known as a urinal, and the woman standing nearby is a patient.

Jacques Philippe Le Bas (1707–83) was perhaps the most famous of the many engravers who have worked on Teniers' masterpieces. His studio in Paris was a hive of engravers in training, and he has been termed " the incarnation of the engraving of the eighteenth century." Pierre François Basan was a contemporary French engraver who also owned a flourishing business in Paris as a printseller. Francesco del Pedro, who has been mentioned above with Basan as an engraver of " Le Grimoire d'Hypocrate," was an Italian engraver of the second half of the eighteenth century. Engravers sometimes added verses or legends to their prints, besides inventing titles for them. For example, an interesting engraving of one of Teniers' lesser alchemical paintings, executed by W. Baillie, bears a quaint legend adapted from *The Alchemist:*

> He's in Belief of Chymistry, so bold,
> If his Dream last, he'll turn the Age to Gold.

Captain William Baillie (1723–1810) was an army officer, born in Ireland, who after his retirement became an outstanding engraver; his extensive works were published by Boydell in 1792 under the title, " A Series of 225 Prints and Etchings after Rembrandt, Teniers, G. Dou, Poussin, and others."

VAN OSTADE

Of Teniers' many contemporaries in art, Adriaen van Ostade (1610–85) was born in the same year, at Haarlem. For a time he worked in the studio of Frans Hals. He achieved fame both as a painter and an etcher, and produced a great profusion of studies of Dutch peasant life and other themes. In alchemical art he is known for his picture "The Alchymist" (1661), which is one of the few classical paintings of an alchemical interior belonging to an English collection, being in the possession of the National Gallery, London.[1] It is a small, delicately executed study of a puffer working in a large rambling laboratory and surrounded by a muddle of apparatus. The laboratory lacks the ordered precision of Teniers' representations, but the puffer is truly at home in it, as it is also his living-room and kitchen. His wife is shown at the far end of this gaunt interior, and two children are leading equally lonely existences in the middle distance. A ladder in the background gives access to a loft which is probably the bedroom of this primitive *ménage*. The scene is one of disorder and penury, summarized by the artist in the words he has inscribed upon a scrap of paper lying on the floor near the puffer: *Oleum et operam perdis*, an echo of Beguin's statement that he had lost both his oil and his labour[2] in certain fruitless experiments. This painting formerly belonged to Sir Robert Peel. It was engraved by Joseph Clayton Bentley (1809–51).

Steen

Among the Dutch artists coming under the influence of Adriaen van Ostade, Steen and Bega are of particular interest from an alchemical point of view. Jan Havickz Steen (1626–79), a celebrated figure painter, was born at Leyden. Like van Ostade, he produced a great profusion of artistic creations. These depicted such subjects as village merriments and weddings, scenes in village taverns and schools, and studies of card-players, doctors, dentists, alchemists, and mountebanks. His best alchemical painting (Plate 23) shows a puffer dropping his last coin into the crucible, with

[1] This picture has been reproduced in A. Findlay's *The Spirit of Chemistry*, London, 1934

[2] Agricola uses the same phrase in *De Re Metallica*, Basel, 1561, p. 2

Plate 26 A Spanish Alchemical Painting (*page 85*)
(Artist unknown)

Plate 27   Chemistry (*page 87*)
(Corbould)

the empty purse lying on the floor between himself and his weeping wife, much after the earlier design of Brueghel. A child and two other figures are seen in the background. A paper pinned to the chimney-piece bears the heading " Teophrastus Paracelsus." Beyond a jug and an ornamented metal mortar in the foreground, little apparatus is shown. In fact, the painting is a study of figures: it throws little light upon laboratory equipment or operations.

A similar idea is interpreted in another of Steen's paintings which is well known in the form of a reversed engraving by Boydell, entitled " The Dutch Chymist." In the original painting, belonging to the Wallace collection, London, a puffer sits at a stone bench, facing right and stirring the contents of a pot with his right hand. Two colleagues stand by him, one of whom reads from a written sheet. In the background, ignored by these three birds of a feather, sits the weeping wife, suckling an infant. This study also is essentially a figure painting. There is a look of grossness about the three men in the foreground. There is no spiritual touch in Steen's figures of alchemists, who appear as rough journeyman puffers; they look like men who would probably beat their wives in the intervals of neglecting them.

Bega

Cornelis Pietersz Bega (1620–64) was born at Haarlem. He became a pupil of van Ostade, whose influence is strongly evident in Bega's style and choice of subjects. The Pope collection, at Cambridge, contained a charming alchemical interior by this artist, painted on a wooden panel and remarkable for the purity of its flesh-tones, its striking light effects, and its delicate tones of heliotrope and blue.[1]

Wijck

Another Dutch artist of this period to achieve a lasting reputation as a painter of alchemical subjects was Thomas

[1] This painting is now in the Fisher collection at Pittsburgh, Pennsylvania

Wijck (Wyck or Wyke), who was born at Beverwijk in 1616 and died at Haarlem in 1677. Like many of his contemporaries, he painted scenes of peasant life and studies of droll characters; he also visited England and painted views of London, including one of the Great Fire of 1666. The alchemist was one of his favourite subjects, and examples of his alchemical interiors have been included in art collections at Amsterdam, the Hague, Brunswick, Dresden, Karlsruhe, and elsewhere. The central figure of the alchemist in Wijck's paintings is very distinctive, and there is usually little variation in this artist's different renderings of the alchemist or his general environment.

Wijck's alchemist has an academic appearance: he seems to be a dilettante and scholar rather than a dour practical worker. He has a short beard and moustache, and wears a kind of doctor's cap; the long loose gown hanging from his shoulders would be distinctly in the way for a labourer in the fire. However, he avoids the hearth, with its charcoal and smoke and dust, and applies himself to the books and manuscripts of which he has accumulated so plentiful a supply. He is usually shown reading at a desk, or standing in the laboratory, surrounded by numerous books and papers, many of which lie crumpled or torn upon the floor. An engraving of one of Wijck's paintings by Victor Texier (1777–1864) is appositely entitled "L'Alchymiste en Méditation" (Plate 24). The properties nearly always include a large globe, a birdcage near the window, and an alligator hanging from the ceiling. Curtains also hang in folds from the ceiling, and cloths and garments are sometimes suspended on drying lines traversing the upper regions of the room. The customary type of hearth, with its fixed bellows and overhanging chimney opening, is absent from these paintings.

Wijck's alchemist is a very gentlemanly type; he is an amateur rather than a professional, and is also something of a recluse, often shown alone, and rarely with more than one other worker in his laboratory. Although he is so tidy and respectable in person, his laboratory is usually in a state of chaos; there are masses of apparatus, much of which has been broken and thrown about the floor in utter disorder, together with a confused medley of pots, papers, and books, diluted copiously with laboratory débris of all kinds, much of which has evidently come down as a heritage from the past. Wijck's alchemist, in contrast to Teniers', inspires no confidence at all as a practical worker.

There is a curious engraving by Pierre Chenu,[1] issued by Basan and entitled "Le Ménage du Chimiste" (Plate 25); it measures 49·8 × 35·6 cm. Although Basan attributed the original to Wijck, the composition has little in common with the alchemical paintings which have just been described. The alchemist of this engraving is an active operator, clad in working attire and offering a sharp contrast to Wijck's passive and meditating alchemist. He is engaged at the usual type of hearth, with chimney opening and fixed bellows. There is no globe, and books are few. Most significant of all, the neglected wife reappears in the background, completely equipped with three children, an infant in a cradle, and an empty purse. Two of the children seem to be searching in an empty store-cupboard, after the manner of Brueghel. The trapdoor in the floor and the ace of diamonds lying nearby are novel features. Certain details suggestive of Wijck may perhaps be traced in this picture; but in its general treatment and spirit the composition is reminiscent of van Ostade or Steen, rather than of Wijck in his usual mood.

The right-hand half of the same subject, containing no figure save that of the alchemist, was issued as a separate engraving under the title "Le Chimiste en Opération," with the attached legend: "Th. Wyck pinx. Gravé par Hormañ de ad Guttenberg. Gravé d'après l'Original tiré du cabinet de M^r. Richard Mead M.D. et Physicien de Sa M. Roiale à Londres. A Paris chez l'Auteur." It is not clear whether Dr. Mead possessed the complete painting or

[1] Chenu was a Parisian engraver of the eighteenth century (1718–80) and a pupil of Le Bas

a slightly altered copy of part of the original.[1] Dr. Richard Mead, F.R.S. (1673-1754), was an outstanding figure in Augustan and early Georgian London. His catholic interests extended from medicine to science, classical learning, and art. He studied in Holland, knew Boerhaave, and was on intimate terms with such men as Newton, Freind, Richard Bentley, and Bishop Burnet. He had a magnificent collection of books, manuscripts, drawings, statuary, and other objects of art: " books for Mead and butterflies for Sloane," wrote Alexander Pope, for whom, incidentally, Mead prescribed asses' milk. In 1727 he became physician to George II. Thomas Major (1720-99), the eminent English engraver, dedicated to Mead, in 1750, one of his several engravings after Teniers, entitled " The Chymist."

Other Dutch Painters

Many other Dutch painters of the seventeenth century occasionally depicted alchemical subjects, without displaying the sustained interest of a Teniers or a Wijck. Among them were Hendrik Zorg, or Sorgh (b. 1621), one of the numerous pupils of Teniers; Hendrik Heerschop (b. 1627); Gabriel Metsu (b. 1630), known for his painting " The Chemist at a Window," in the Louvre; Frans van Mieris (b. 1635); and Jan Luyken (b. 1649). Justus Gustav van Bentum, of Leyden (b. 1670), departed from the usual type of alchemical subjects in his painting of an explosion in an alchemist's laboratory, the light effects being shown vividly on the canvas, after the manner of Rembrandt, by exposing a preliminary coating of sienna at the illuminated points.[2] This artist was a pupil of Gottfried Schalken, of Dordrecht (b. 1643), who specialized in candlelight paintings; Schalken, in turn, had studied light effects of this kind as a pupil of the celebrated Gerard Dou (b. 1613), an artist who also included some subjects of alchemical interest among his many superb paintings.

[1] An old painting of this picture on a wooden panel (43 × 35 cm.) has been reported from Buenos Aires; this bears the initials " D. T.," and does not include anything to the left of the cradle. The implied attribution to David Teniers is not borne out by the character of the composition.
[2] The original painting is in the Fisher collection, Pittsburgh

Plate 28 Hocus Pocus or Searching for the Philosophers Stone (*page 87*)
(Rowlandson)

Plate 29 The Discovery of Phosphorus (*page 88*)
(Wright)

THE ALCHEMIST IN ART

A Spanish Alchemical Painting

Our pictorial ideas of alchemists and alchemical laboratories have been derived mainly from the rich array of such subjects issuing from the Flemish and Dutch schools. Representations of alchemists and their operations by artists of other countries, such as Alessandro Magnasco in Italy, are fewer and not so well known. So firmly established is the Flemish and Dutch tradition that such paintings have an exotic appearance. An example is shown in Plate 26, which is a reproduction of a painting [1] of uncertain attribution, probably of Spanish origin and dating from the first half of the seventeenth century. When found, some years ago, in a dealer's shop, this painting was so black as to be completely undiscernible. Treatment with a damp sponge revealed a suggestion of a figure with a wooden leg in the upper part of the canvas. This observation pointed to the possibility of an alchemical subject, which was borne out when the painting was carefully cleaned.

The painting measures about 38 by 28 inches. The background has a rich brown tone, and bright tints of red, blue, light brown and olive-green are the outstanding colours in the garments of the figures with which the canvas is crowded. The great congestion in the laboratory differentiates it in a marked manner from the alchemical interiors of the painters of the Low Countries; the domestic motive is absent, and other striking differences are revealed in the attire of the laborants and the nature of their apparatus. The swarthy countenances and turban-like headgear impart a Moorish look to some of the figures. The apparatus is limited to simple retorts, flasks, and bowls, together with a pestle and mortar in the bottom right-hand corner. Two furnaces are shown on the left, one being built in an alcove.

The materials in use seem to be as simple and circumscribed as the apparatus. Two central figures at a long table on the right are transferring a bright red powder, probably cinnabar, from one retort to another. A partly clad figure

[1] The original is in the St. Andrews alchemical collection

kneeling on the floor in front of the table handles a sheaf of grain. The third figure from the left, engaged at the furnace in the foreground, holds what appears to be a bunch of wheat-heads in one hand. His right-hand neighbour is pouring a liquid into a bowl, and so is the tall figure (clad in red) in the middle of the composition. A monkey in an erect posture in the left foreground holds a platter of material resembling sliced bananas more than anything else.

Of the numerous figures, twelve are assembled around the table; the chairman, who has a pronounced Moorish look, is consulting one of the five books shown in the painting. The ties are clearly shown on the front edges of the book held by the figure reclining on the floor. Behind the chairman a laborant laden with apparatus stands in an elevated recess. To the left of the table there is a group of three figures; four others form an intimate and attractive cluster around the furnace in the foreground; there are four in the alcove and two on the balcony above. In addition there are the two symbolical figures in the panel—possibly Saturn and Luna (as in the Ninth Key of Basilius)—and the monkey. The total number of figures in this remarkable composition is twenty-nine.

The glass apparatus, including a supply of spare retorts and flasks arranged on shelves to the right of the panel, is skilfully indicated by the use of thin streaks of white paint representing the high lights. The panel has a light blue background serving to detach it effectively from the dark brown surround.

Later Alchemical Paintings

With the decline of alchemy in the eighteenth century, the alchemical theme in art lost a great deal of its force and popular appeal. Nevertheless, the artistic tradition of alchemy was kept alive in such paintings as Joseph Wright's imaginative and romantic treatment of " The Discovery of Phosphorus." A generation later, a painting little known, although of particular significance in chemistry, marked the opening of the nineteenth century. Conceived by an English artist, Richard Corbould (1757–1831), soon after the overthrow of phlogiston, it appeared in the interregnum between Lavoisier and Dalton as an apt symbolization of the change from the ancient art of alchemy to the modern science of chemistry (Plate 27).

Chemistry, shown in the guise of an attractive damsel, is hesitating between the old and the new. She stands at the parting of the ways. But it is clear which path she will take; for although her left hand lingers caressingly on the old philosopher's shoulder, all her attention is given to the young chemist who is demonstrating to her the preparation of oxygen. This striking painting, entitled " Chemistry," was shown at the Royal Academy in 1805; it was engraved in mezzotint by John Chapman (1772–1816).

Even caricatures of alchemy did not end with the Dutch and Flemish schools, for so late as 1800 Thomas Rowlandson (1756–1827) issued an amusing drawing in colour (Plate 28), entitled " Hocus Pocus or Searching for the Philosophers Stone," in which the errant and dashing laboratory assistant (who would seem from his attire to be a gentleman volunteer) appears to have outstripped his master in the search for the universal catalyst. The laboratory is well equipped with the usual properties, including even a fish suspended from the ceiling. A sketch on the wall provides a hit of contemporary interest at " Count Caliostro Discoverer of the Philosopher's Stone," who is handling some bulging bags of gold.

After the eighteenth century, paintings of alchemical interest ceased to have first-hand historical value. The alchemical motif, however, has continued to act occasionally as a source of inspiration to painters down to the present day, and considerable artistic merit is evident in some of the modern compositions. Two representative examples of different types may be seen in " Rudolphe chez son Alchemiste,"[1] by Wenceslas Brozik (1851–1900), a Bohemian historical

[1] Reproduced, for example, in H. C. Bolton's *The Follies of Science at the Court of Rudolph II, 1576–1612*, Milwaukee, 1904, and C. J. S. Thompson's *The Lure and Romance of Alchemy*, London, 1932

painter, and "Weary of the Search,"[1] a sympathetic study of an alchemist who has fallen asleep in his laboratory, by the American painter, Elihu Vedder (1836–1923).

WRIGHT OF DERBY

One of the most famous alchemical paintings of the eighteenth century is "The Discovery of Phosphorus" (Plate 29), by the English painter, Joseph Wright, of Derby (1734–97). In essence, Wright continued the tradition of Schalken and van Bentum by painting the effects of light. He was fond of placing a strong source of light in a central part of his composition and tracing the high lights and shadows created in this way: in such studies the figures stand out in strong relief. He began experimenting with candlelight and firelight pieces, eventually producing such masterpieces as "Three Persons viewing the Gladiator by Candlelight" (1765), "A Philosopher giving that Lecture on the Orrery in which a Lamp is put in the place of the Sun" (1766), "An Experiment on a Bird in the Air Pump" (1768), and "The Discovery of Phosphorus" (1771), together with "A Blacksmith's Shop," "An Iron Forge," "Miss Kitty Dressing," and other subjects. Of these, "The Discovery of Phosphorus" and "The Orrery" belong to the Derby Corporation Art Gallery, and "The Air Pump" to the National Gallery, London.

Some of these paintings were beautifully engraved in mezzotint—a process to which they are peculiarly responsive—by the renowned English engravers, William Pether (1731–1795), Richard Earlom (1743–1822), and Valentine Green (1739–1813). The early impressions, in particular, are distinguished by an exquisite velvety quality. This work owed much to the incentive of John Boydell (1719–1804), a skilled and energetic engraver who raised English engraving of the eighteenth century to a very high level, and incidentally became Lord Mayor of London towards the close of the century (1791).

[1] This painting hangs in the Brooklyn Museum

Wright's interest in science finds repeated expression in his paintings, notably in "The Orrery" and "The Discovery of Phosphorus." In the first of these subjects the central figure is a philosopher, in the second an alchemist.

The venerable philosopher of "The Orrery" stands in the mid-background of the composition, behind the instrument, from which vantage-point he demonstrates the motion of the planets to an audience of seven members. The chiaroscuro reveals him as a commanding figure in a handsome brocaded gown; his head is massive and intellectual, his face furrowed and seamed with lines of thought. Below his pointing right hand the full glare of the hidden lamp lights up the smooth cherubic countenances of two children, who peer intently between the brass hoops of the orrery at the moving models of the planets. Facing them in the foreground, a third childish figure, eclipsing the lamp, is shown in darkly silhouetted outline. To right and left the light streams away to disclose four other figures, each characteristically intent upon the demonstration.

The full title of Wright's alchemical painting runs as follows: "The Alchymist in Search of the Philosopher's Stone discovers Phosphorus and prays for the successful Conclusion of his Operation, as was the custom of the ancient Chymical Astrologers."

The scene is a dark, vaulted room, at night, in the crypt of an ancient building. Here, an alchemist, after "long labour unto agéd breath," is making yet another distillation, in the midst of a gloom lightened only by faint moonbeams from without and the feebler rays of a candle from within. The moon rides ever higher above the lofty mullioned window, revealing its tracery in stark outline. Midnight draws nigh. The agéd adept—for he is no mere puffer—watches and prays.

Suddenly a dim glow begins to steal into the dark receiver. The alchemist and his two acolytes shade their eyes and watch the strange sight with wonder and awe. The glow lives, and grows, and spreads, till it illumines every corner of that drear and dunky chamber with an unearthly light. . . . The ancient alchemist raises heavenwards eyes that have long since grown dim with gazing on earthly fires. It is surely his *Nunc Dimittis* that has been written by Victor Hugo :

"The sun is born of fire, the moon of the sun. Fire is the soul of the Great All, its elementary atoms are diffused and constantly flowing by an infinity of currents throughout the universe. At the points where these currents cross each other in the heavens they produce light ; at their points of intersection in the earth they produce gold. Light—gold ; it is the same thing—fire in its concrete state. . . . What ! this light that bathes my hand is gold ! All that is necessary is to condense by a certain law these same atoms dilated by certain other laws ! . . . Flamel considers it simpler to operate with terrestrial fire. Flamel ! there's predestination in the very name ! *Flamma !* yes, fire—that is all. The diamond exists already in the charcoal, gold in fire—But how to extract it ? . . . What ! I hold in my hand the magic hammer ! " . . . *Nunc dimittis, Domine !*

REFERENCES

1. BRYAN, M., *Bryan's Dictionary of Painters and Engravers*, new edition, revised and enlarged under the supervision of G. C. Williamson, 5 vols., London, 1903–1905
2. CHAUCER, G., *Canterbury Tales*, edited by A. Burrell [1908], Everyman's Library, London and New York
3. FERGUSON, J., *Bibliotheca Chemica*, 2 vols., Glasgow, 1906
4. FORMAN, S., *The Autobiography and Personal Diary of Dr. Simon Forman* (from MSS. in the Ashmolean Museum, Oxford), editor, J. O. Halliwell, London, 1849
5. HARTLAUB, G. F., "Arcana Artis," *Zeitschrift für Kunstgeschichte*, 1938, *6*, 289
6. HUGO, V., *Notre-Dame of Paris*, translated from the French of Victor Hugo, and edited by E. Gosse, London, 1908
7. JONSON, B., *The Alchemist*, The King's Library edition, London, 1903
8. JUNG, C. G., *Psychologie und Alchemie*, Zürich, 1944
9. LIEBIG, J. von, *Familiar Letters in Chemistry*, 4th edition, London, 1859
10. PARTINGTON, J. R., *A Short History of Chemistry*, London, 1937
11. READ, JOHN, *Prelude to Chemistry: An Outline of Alchemy, its Literature and Relationships*, 2nd edition, London, 1939
12. *Idem, Humour and Humanism in Chemistry*, London, 1947; this work is a sequel to (11) above
13. *Idem, A Text-Book of Organic Chemistry, Historical, Structural, and Economic* (chap. iii), London, 1947
14. *Idem*, "The Pope Collection of Alchemical Paintings and Engravings," *Nature*, 1941, *147*, 243
15. READ, JOHN HINTON (Jan), "Some Alchemical Engravings," *The Burlington Magazine*, 1944, *85*, 239
16. THOMSON, JAMES, *The City of Dreadful Night* (1874), canto xxi
17. *The Harleian Miscellany*, vol. 7, London, 1811: NICCOLS, R., "Sir Thomas Overbury's Vision" (originally printed, 1616); "The Five Years of King James" (originally printed, 1643).

GLOSSARY

This list is confined to alchemical terms quoted in the text without explanation. For terms explained in the text, reference should be made to the Index.

Ablution, the process of washing a solid with a liquid, usually water.

Alembic, the upper part of a still, otherwise a still-head (also *limbeck*, or *helm*—from its resemblance to a helmet). The term is sometimes wrongly used to denote a complete still (see under *Cucurbite*).

Aludel, a pear-shaped earthenware bottle, open at both ends, used as a condenser in sublimation processes.

Aqua regia, a mixture of *aqua fortis* (nitric acid) and *spiritus salis* or spirit of salt (hydrochloric acid), so called because of its solvent action on gold, the alchemical King. It was known to the Islamic alchemists, and later Glauber prepared it by distilling common salt with *aqua fortis*.

Aqua vitae, aqueous alcohol concentrated by one or more distillations.

Argent-vive, quicksilver, mercury; silver in a "quick," vivified, or mobile state.

Athanor, an alchemical furnace, sometimes regarded as an incubatory furnace, under the name of the House of the Chick (*i.e.* Philosopher's Stone).

Balneo, bath (of water, sand, ashes, etc.), capable of being heated.

Bolt-head, a round-bottomed flask with a long neck (also *matrass*).

Brimstone, sulphur.

Calx vive, quicklime.

Ceration, the mollification, or softening, of a hard material, to bring it into a waxy or still more fluid state.

Circulator, a closed vessel, or double vessel, permitting of a primitive form of reflux distillation.

Cohobation, the pouring back of a distillate from its residue, or faeces, followed by redistillation.

GLOSSARY

Croslet, crucible.

Cucurbite, the lower part of a still, containing the original liquid. This was made of earthenware or glass, and was also known as a *gourd*, on account of its shape.

Cupel, a small shallow cup or dish made of bone-ash or other porous and infusible material.

Cupellation, the process of heating in a cupel in a current of air, as in the refining of silver and gold.

Fixation, the process of depriving a substance of its volatility or mobility; defined by Geber as "the convenient disposing of a fugitive thing, to abide and sustain the fire." Glauber summarized the preparation of the Philosopher's Stone in the following " sutable Poesie ":

> Dissolve the Fixt, and make the Fixed fly,
> The Flying fix, and then live happily.

Gripe's-egg, griffin's egg: an allusion to the egg-shaped Vessel of Hermes. The griffin, being half lion and half eagle, was a symbol of the conjunction of the fixed and volatile principles or the two-fold mercurial matter.

Helm, the upper part of a still (see under *Alembic*).

Lunara, the plant, lunary or moonwort (*Botrychium lunara*), also known to the alchemists as *Martagon*.

Lute, a cement used in sealing apertures and joints of apparatus.

Magnesia, a vague term comprising several mineral substances, including pyrites, magnetite, pyrolusite, and possibly magnesia.

Markasits, pyrites.

Martagon, see under *Lunara*.

Merds, excreta.

Mizerion, the plant, *Daphne mezereum*.

Multiplication, commonly synonymous with transmutation; but meaning sometimes (especially among the adepts) a concentration of the transmuting power, or an increase of the amount, of the Stone as obtained in its pristine form.

Pelican, a circulatory vessel with two side-arms, having a fancied resemblance in shape to the bird after which it was named.

GLOSSARY

Projection, the final process of gold-making, effected by throwing the Stone, or powder of projection (in very small amount) upon the hot molten metal to be transmuted.

Sandifer, dross from molten glass, forming a scum.

Solution, the process of dissolving a solid in a liquid; defined by Geber as "the reduction of a dry thing into water."

Sublimation, the vaporization of a solid without fusion, followed by condensation of the vapour in the solid form upon a cool surface; defined by Geber as "the elevation of a dry thing by fire, with adherency to its vessel."

Tutits, zinc carbonate or oxide.

Ulen Spiegel, a German prototype of boorish and malicious buffoonery, who is said to have lived in the early fourteenth century (usually *Till Eulenspiegel*, or "Owl-glass").

Vitriall, a glistening crystalline body, such as *white vitriol* (zinc sulphate), *green vitriol* (ferrous sulphate), and *blue vitriol* (copper sulphate). Basil Valentine mentioned "a glorious vitriol" (copper acetate) obtained by extracting verdigris with distilled vinegar.

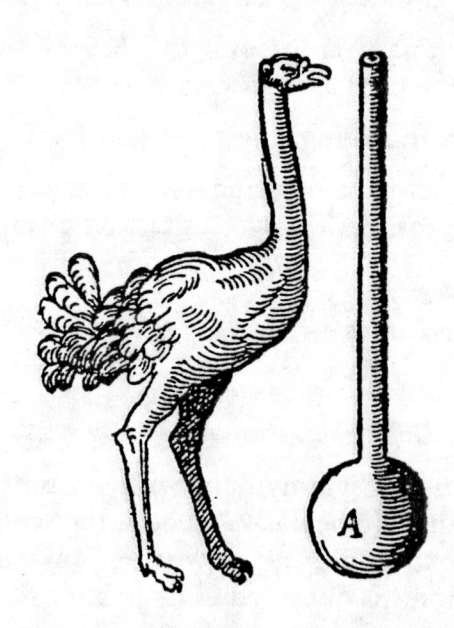

GLOSSARY

Croslet, crucible.

Cucurbite, the lower part of a still, containing the original liquid. This was made of earthenware or glass, and was also known as a *gourd*, on account of its shape.

Cupel, a small shallow cup or dish made of bone-ash or other porous and infusible material.

Cupellation, the process of heating in a cupel in a current of air, as in the refining of silver and gold.

Fixation, the process of depriving a substance of its volatility or mobility; defined by Geber as " the convenient disposing of a fugitive thing, to abide and sustain the fire." Glauber summarized the preparation of the Philosopher's Stone in the following " sutable Poesie " :

> Dissolve the Fixt, and make the Fixed fly,
> The Flying fix, and then live happily.

Gripe's-egg, griffin's egg : an allusion to the egg-shaped Vessel of Hermes. The griffin, being half lion and half eagle, was a symbol of the conjunction of the fixed and volatile principles or the two-fold mercurial matter.

Helm, the upper part of a still (see under *Alembic*).

Lunara, the plant, lunary or moonwort (*Botrychium lunara*), also known to the alchemists as *Martagon*.

Lute, a cement used in sealing apertures and joints of apparatus.

Magnesia, a vague term comprising several mineral substances, including pyrites, magnetite, pyrolusite, and possibly magnesia.

Markasits, pyrites.

Martagon, see under *Lunara*.

Merds, excreta.

Mizerion, the plant, *Daphne mezereum*.

Multiplication, commonly synonymous with transmutation ; but meaning sometimes (especially among the adepts) a concentration of the transmuting power, or an increase of the amount, of the Stone as obtained in its pristine form.

Pelican, a circulatory vessel with two side-arms, having a fancied resemblance in shape to the bird after which it was named.

GLOSSARY

Projection, the final process of gold-making, effected by throwing the Stone, or powder of projection (in very small amount) upon the hot molten metal to be transmuted.

Sandifer, dross from molten glass, forming a scum.

Solution, the process of dissolving a solid in a liquid; defined by Geber as "the reduction of a dry thing into water."

Sublimation, the vaporization of a solid without fusion, followed by condensation of the vapour in the solid form upon a cool surface; defined by Geber as "the elevation of a dry thing by fire, with adherency to its vessel."

Tutits, zinc carbonate or oxide.

Ulen Spiegel, a German prototype of boorish and malicious buffoonery, who is said to have lived in the early fourteenth century (usually *Till Eulenspiegel*, or "Owl-glass").

Vitriall, a glistening crystalline body, such as *white vitriol* (zinc sulphate), *green vitriol* (ferrous sulphate), and *blue vitriol* (copper sulphate). Basil Valentine mentioned "a glorious vitriol" (copper acetate) obtained by extracting verdigris with distilled vinegar.

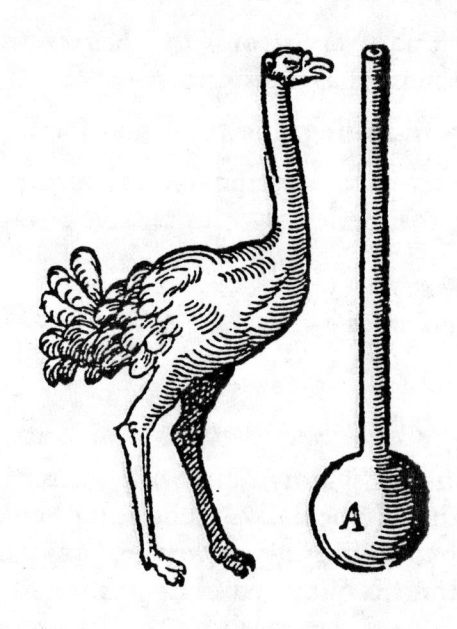

INDEX

Acrostic, 20
Adepts, 13, 14, 89
Agricola, 24, 68, 80
Agrippa, 58
Air, 38
Albertus Magnus, 24
Alchemical apparatus, 15, 17, 33, 62, 65, 71, 85; inscriptions, 70, 71; literature, 16, 25; manuscripts, 16, 23; materials, 13, 34, 71; operations, 13, 65; symbolism, 16, 17, 18, 19, 20, 56, 59; terms, 33, 42, 65, 92; theory, 3; triangle, 7
Alchemist, The, viii, ix, 11, 14, 27, 38 *et seq.*, Pls. *10, 11, 12*
Alchemists, 2, 23, 24, 59, 64, 69; in art, 56 *et seq.*; in literature, 25 *et seq.*
Alchemy, nature, 1, 3; origin, 2
Alcohol, 50, *see also* Aqua vitae
Alembic, 15, 33, 62, 76
Althotas, 27
Altus, 20
Amphitheatrum Sapientiae Æternae, ix (*Pl. 17*), 69
Amulets, 58
Androgyne, 17, 22
Antimony, 19
Antiquary, The, 27
Apparatus, alchemical, 15, 17, 33, 62, 65, 71, 85
Aqua vitae, 13, 52, 53
Architecture, 56
Aristotle, 3, 4
Arnold of Villanova, 38
Ars Destillatoria, x
Ashmole, 15, 22
Assaying, 26
Astrolabe, 29
Astrology, 1, 9, 15, 19, 47, 49, 71
Atalanta Fugiens, viii (*Pls. 2, 6*), 11, 21, 22, 68
Athanor, 15, 70, *Pl. 3*
Audinet, viii (*Pl. 9*)
Aureum Vellus, 25
Azoth, 71

Bacon, R., 6, 24
Baillie, 79
Balance, 58, 59
Balsamo, 27
Balzac, 28, 69
Barchusen, viii (*Pl. 3*)
Basan, ix (*Pl. 25*), 74, 78, 79, 83
Basilius. *See* Basil Valentine
Basil Valentine, 10, 18, 19, 86, *Pl. 4*
Bath, 60
Bear, 17, 24
Bega, 81
Beguin, 80
Bellows, 13, 15, 29, 33, 64, 65, 71, 76, 77, 78
Bentley, J. C., 80
Bentley, R., 84
Besançon, Hugh of, 71
Bibliography, 91
Bibliotheca Chemica, 16
Biringuccio, 68
Body, 7, 8
Bolton, 87
Born, Inigo, 27
Boydell, 79, 81, 88
Boyle, 8
Brimstone, 34, 38
Brozik, 87
Brueghel, 59, 63, 65, 68, 69, 72, 75, 78, 81, 83, *Pl. 15*
Brunschwick, 23, 24
Bryan, 91
Bulfinch, ix, *Pl. 13*
Burrell, 30

Cagliostro, 27, 87
Caloric, 6
Calx, 13, 14
Canon's Yeoman's Tale, 27, 29, 39
Canterbury Tales, 29
Caricature, 65, 75
Caulfield, ix (*Pl. 13*)
Cellini, 68
Chaldea, 9
Chapman, x (*Pl. 27*), 87
Chaucer, viii, xii, 9, 27, 28, 29, 39, 57, 59, 91, *Pl. 7*

95

INDEX

Chemistry, modern, 8, 9, 24, 87
Chenu, ix (*Pl. 25*), 83
Chick, 21
Child's play, 60, 78
China, 2, 3
Chirico, 21
Christian mystery, 23, 56
Circle, 20
Cock, H., ix (*Pl. 15*), 63
Coleridge, 39
Colour in alchemy, 17, 18, 45, 56, 58
Colours of the Great Work, 12, 45
Combustion, 5, 9
Compasses, 58, 59, 60, 61
Compound of Alchymie, The, 14
Contraries, Doctrine of, 3, 7
Copper plate. *See* Engravings
Corbould, x, 87, *Pl. 27*
Cosmopolite, the, 26
Cracow, 26
Cranach, 57, 60, 61
Cripple, 18, 60
Crocodile, 75
Croslet, 33, 36, 37, 44
Crow, 12, 17, 46
Crucible, 13, 15, 19, 23, 33, 58, 62, 63, 65, 75, 80
Cupel, 19, 65
Cupids, 78

Dalton, 87
Damian, 13
de Bry, 21, 68, 69
De Distillatione, x
Dee, 40, 42, 47
de Givry, 72
De Natura Rerum, 64
Dentists, 80
De Remediis, 62
De Re Metallica, 80
de Vries, 70
Dienheim, 47
Doctors, 64, 75, 79, 80
Dog, 58, 60
Dou, 75, 79, 84
Dove, 17
Doyle, Conan, 28
Dragon, 17, 38, 71
Drury Lane, 41
Dürer, ix, 22, 57 *et seq.*, *Pl. 14*
Dumas, Alexandre, 27
Dutch painters, 68, 72, 80, 84, 85

Eagle, 20
Earlom, 88

Earth, 3, 8
Egg. *See* Philosopher's Egg
Egypt, 2, 3, 61
Elaboratory, 77
Elementa Chemiae, viii (*Pl. 3*)
Elements, 3, 9, 10, 12, 16, 17, 20, 58
Elixir of Life, 4, 29
Emerald Table, 16, 19
Engravings, 11, 20, 21, 63, 66, 74, 79, 81
Epicoene, 47
Esoteric alchemy, 13, 17, 29, 60
Essex, Countess of, 48
Exoteric alchemy, 13, 17, 29, 38

Fat, 8
Faustus, 71, 72
Feminine principle, 7, 8, 10, 17, 19
Ferchl, 66
Ferguson, 16, 91
Figures of Abraham, 18
Findlay, 80
Fire, 3, 5, 6, 15, 19, 21, 58, 59, 90
Fish, 75, 77, 87
Fisher Collection, 76, 81, 84
Fitzer, 68
Five Elements, 3
Fixed principle, 8, 17, 20
Flamel, 18, 27, 47, 56, 90
Flemish painters, 62, 68, 72, 85
Flowers, 19
Forman, ix, 27, 40, 47 *et seq.*, 91, *Pl. 13*
Four Elements, 3, 10
Frescoes, 18, 56
Fruit, 10, 18, 22
Furnaces, 13, 15, 64, 65, 66, *Pl. 3*

Galle, P., ix (*Pl. 16*), 66
Galle, T., ix (*Pl. 15*), 63
Garrick, ix, 41, *Pl. 12*
Geber, 5
Gianni, ix (*Pl. 24*)
Glauber, 8, 24
Godfrey, ix (*Pl. 13*)
Goethe, 4
Gold and gold making, 1, 4, 6, 9, 13, 14, 25, 27, 30, 59, 71, 79, 90
Grail, 19
Grand Magisterium, 12, 43
Great Work, the, 7, 12, 15, 18, 20, 45, 56, 58, 60, 61, 70, *Pl. 5*
Green, V., 88
Greek influence, 3, 4, 9, 10

96

INDEX

Grindstone, 61, 77
Gunpowder, 67, *Pl. 16*

Hals, 79
Ham, Land of, 2
Hammer, 58, 90
Harleian Miscellany, The, 48, 91
Hartlaub, 60, 91
Heavy water, 18, 59
Heerschop, 84
Helicon, 12
Helvetius, 27, 47
Hermaphroditic figures, 17
Hermes, 2, 16, 20, 38, 63
Hermetic androgyne, 17 ; art, 2 ; mythology, 11, 23 ; Stream, 18, 59 ; Vessel, 14, 15, 19, 21, 45, 70, *Pl. 3*
"Hocus Pocus," x, 87, *Pl. 28*
Holmyard, 67
Honthorst, viii (*Pl. 9*)
Hoop, 20, 60, 61
Hound, 61
Hour-glass, 58, 59, 65
House of the Chick, 75
Hugo, 56, 71, 90, 91
Humours, 12, 58
Hylozoism, 9
Hypostatical principles, 7

Iatrochemistry, 7
India, 3
Infants, 7, 60, 61
Inflammable substances, 5, 6, 8
Iron, 9, 21
Islam, 2
Italy, 25, 63, 67, 85

Jabir, 5
Jacob, 59
James IV, 13
Jonson, Ben, viii, 11, 14, 27, 28, 39, 47, 69, 91, *Pl. 9*
Jorma, 77
Jung, 1, 20, 91
Jupiter, 9, 11, 12, 19, 58, 59

Kelly, 42
Keys, 61
Khem, 2
Khunrath, ix (*Pl. 17*), 23, 69, 71
King, 17, 19
Kingsley, 24
Kitchen, 63, 65
Kronos, 59

Laboratories, alchemical, 62, 65, 66, 69, 71, 72, 75, 76, 85
Ladder, 59
Lamp, 61
La Recherche de l'Absolu, 28
Lavoisier, 87
Lead, 9, 19, 25, 59, 60
Le Bas, 79, 83
"Le Grimoire d'Hypocrate," ix (*Pl. 21*), 74, 77, 78, 79
Le Plaisir des Fous, 78
Libavius, 8, 24
Liber de Arte Distillandi, 23
Liebig, 1, 5, 75, 91
Life, 1, 2, 9
Light effects, 88, 89
Lion, 17, 19, 20
Little Work, 12
Longevity, 4
Lorieux, ix (*Pl. 19*), 75
Ludus puerorum, 60, 78
Lully, 7
Luna, 9, 19, 38, 58, 86
Lunary, 12, 13, 93
Luyken, 84

Macrocosm, 9
Magic, 1, 10, 48, 49, 52, 53, 57, 71, 72
Magic square, 58
Magnasco, 85
Magnesia, 7, 70
Magnus, Albertus, 24
Maier, Count M., viii (*Pls. 1, 2, 4, 6*), 11, 21, 23, 43, 68
Major, 77, 84
Marriage, 19
Mars, 9, 19, 21, 58
Masculine principle, 7, 8, 10, 17, 19
Matham, 72
Mead, Dr. R., 83, 84
Medicine, 4, 7, 15, 52, 64
Melancholy, 49, 59, 60, 62, 70
"Melencolia," ix, 22, 57 *et seq.*, *Pl. 14*
Mémoires d'un Médecin, 27
Menstruum, 14, 17, 59
Mercury, 6, 8, 10, 19, 20, 38, 58, 70
Merian, 68
Metals, 5–7, 9, 10, 20, 58, 59, 90
Metsu, 84
Mezzotints, 21, 88

97

INDEX

Micah Clarke, 28
Michon, ix (*Pl. 19*), 75
Microcosm, 9, 70
Milton, 61
Moisture, 60
Monkey, 78, 86
Moon, 9, 12, 17, 19, 20, 90
Moon-tree, 18, 60
Moor's head, 76
Mortification, 13, 14
Muir, 5
Multiplication, 9, 14
Munchausen, Baron, 27
Music, 11, 60, 70
Mutus Liber, 20, 59
Mysticism, 7, 8, 23, 56, 57, 69
Mythology, 1, 11, 23, 43, 60

Nails, 58
Necromancy, 27, 41, 49, 53
Niccols, 48, 49
Norton, Thomas, 11, 12, 13, 14, 15, 19, 23, 25, 29, 33
Notre-Dame de Paris, 56, 71
Number, 10, 57, 58, 70

Occleve, viii (*Pl. 7*)
Occultism, 1
Œdipus Tyrannus, 39
Operations of the Great Work, 13, 15
Oratory, 71, *Pl. 17*
Orb, 20
Ordinall of Alchimy, 13, 19, 23, 25
Ostrich, 17, 94
Overbury, Sir Thomas, 48
Oxidation, 14
Oxygen, 87

Paracelsus, 7, 8, 14, 42, 64, 65, 81
Paris, 56, 71
Partington, 91
Peacock's tail, 12, 19, 69
Pedro, del, 73, 79
Pelican, vi, 44, 46, 93
Pepys, 39
Perrenelle, 18, 27
Pether, x (*Pl. 29*), 88
Petrarch, 62
Philosopher's Egg, 15, 21, 61, *Pl. 6*;
— Stone, 4, 5, 6, 7, 10, 12, 16, 20, 21, 29, 31, 36, 38, 41, 53, 54, 56, 58, 59, 61, 70, 87, 89
Philosophy, 1, 69

Phlegma, 8
Phlogiston, 8, 87
Phoenix, 17
Phosphorus, 88, 89, *Pl. 29*
Plane, 58
Planets, 17, 19
Plato, 4, 58
Polyhedron, 58, 59
Ponteleone, 26, 67
Pope, Alexander, 84
Pope, Sir W. J., 78, 81
Porta, x
Poussin, 79
Poverty of alchemists, 24, 63, 64, 80
Powder of projection, 4, 29, 36, 54; *see also* Philosopher's Stone
Prague, 11, 40
Prayer, 70
Precepts of Hermes, 16, 61
Prima materia, 4
Primitive materials, 14, 17
Principles of natural bodies, 7, 8, 10
Projection, 14
Proximate materials, 19
Psychology, 1, 20
Puffers, 13, 23, 29, 64, 69, 80, 81
"Pulvis Pyrius," 67, *Pl. 16*
Purse, 61, 63, 78, 81, 83
Putrefaction, 9, 13, 14
Pythagoras, 10, 11, 57, 58, 70

Qualities, 3
Queen, 17, 19
Quentin Durward, 27
Quicksilver, 6, 7, 9, 13, 14, 34, 36, 37
Quidhampton, 49, 52
Quintessence, 4, 10

Rainbow, 12, 23, 58, 69
Raphael, 21
Raspe, 27
Read, J., 91
Read, J. H., 21, 22, 91
Rebis, 17
Red Tincture, 4, 12
Reduction, 14
Regeneration, 9, 60, 61
Rejuvenation, 20
Religion, 1, 9, 18, 23, 56, 69, 70
Rembrandt, 71, 72, 79, 84
Renaissance art, 21, 60

INDEX

Resurrection, 14
Reversed engravings, 74
Rhea, 11
Rink, viii, 77
Ripley, 14, 56, 70
Rochester, Viscount, 48
Rowlandson, x, 87, *Pl. 28*
Rubens, 73
Rudolph II, 11, 40, 87

St. Andrews Collection, vi, viii, x, 77, 85
Saintsbury, 28
Salamander, 75
Sal ammoniac, 13, 34
Salt, 7, 8, 10
Sanguis Agni, 44
Sarum, 50, 52
Saturn, 9, 11, 12, 19, 22, 54, 58, 59, 60, 86; mysticism, 18, 19, 59, 61, *Pl. 2*
Saw, 58
Sceptical Chymist, The, 8
Schalken, 84, 88
Schwarz, Berthold, 67
Scott, Sir W., 27
Scythe, 19
Secretioris Naturae Secretorum Scrutinium Chymicum, viii (*Pl. 6*), 22
Seeds, 9, 10, 20, 31
Serpent, 17, 20, 61
Seton, 26
Signatures, Doctrine of, 12
Silver, 9, 13, 14, 19, 26, 34, 36, 37, 59
Soap-bubble, 61, 78
Sol, 9, 19, 38, 58
Somerset, Earl of, 48
Sophic mercury, 6, 7, 9, 14, 17, 38, 59, 71; sulphur, 6, 7, 9, 14, 17, 38, 58, 59
Sorgh, 84
Souffleurs, 13, 23, 29
Soul, 7, 8
Spagyrists, 64
Spanish painting, 85, *Pl. 26*
Sphere, 58, 60, 61
Spheres, music of, 11
Spirit, 7, 8
Splendor Solis, 18, 25, 26, 59, 60
Square, 20
Stars, 20, 71
Steen, ix, 78, 80, 81, 83, *Pl. 23*
Stills, 17, 75, 76

Stirling Castle, 13
Stolcius, viii (*Pl. 5*), x
Stork, 17, 55
Stradanus, ix, 66, 67 68, 69, 72, *Pl. 16*
Strassburg, 23
Straub, ix (*Pl. 20*), 77
Sublimation, 17
Sulphur, 6, 8, 10, 20, 70
Sulphur-mercury Theory, 5, 7, *Pl. 1*
Sun, 9, 17, 19, 90
Sun-god, 9
Sun-tree, 18, 60
Surrealism, 21
Süssenguth, 66
Swan, 17, 54
Swinburne, 39
Sword, 21
Symbola Aureae Mensae Duodecim Nationum, viii (*Pl. 1*), 21
Symbolism, 16–20, 56, 59

Tabula Smaragdina, 16, 19
Talismans, 20, 58
Taoism, 2
Temperaments, 57
Teniers, viii, ix, xi, 15, 59, 61, 66, 73 *et seq.*, 84, *Pls. 18, 19, 20, 21, 22*
Texier, ix (*Pl. 24*), 82
Theatrum Chemicum Britannicum, 15, 22
Thompson, C. J. S., 87
Thomson, J., 61, 91
Thoth, 2
Tin, 9, 13, 26
Tincture, 4, 10, 12, 26
Tingeing, 6, 26
Tom Jones, 39
Transmutation, 1, 4, 6, 24, 26, 29
Transmuting powder, 4, 29, 36, 54
Triangle, 7, 71
Tria prima, 7, 10, 17, 19
Trinity, 23, 56, 70
Tripus Aureus, viii (*Pl. 4*)
Trismegistos. *See* Hermes
Trismosin, 18, 25, 26, 47, 67
Trostspiegel, 62
Turba Philosophorum, 69
Turner, Mrs., 48
Twelve Keys, 19
Two-Thing, 17

INDEX

Ulen Spiegel, 44, 94
Unity of matter, 4, 9, 16
Urinals, 15, 33, 79

Valentine. *See* Basil Valentine
van Bentum, 84, 88
van der Doort, ix (*Pl. 17*)
van der Straet. *See* Stradanus
van Helmont, 8, 27, 47
van Mieris, 84
van Ostade, 78, 79, 80, 81, 83
Vase of Hermes, 14, 19, 58, 61, 70, *Pl. 3*
Vaughan, 22
Vedder, 88
Venice, 26, 67
Venus, 9, 19, 58
Village scenes, 66, 72, 73, 80, 82
Vinegar, 13, 44
Viridarium Chymicum, viii (*Pls. 1, 4, 5*), x
Vitriol, 20
Vivification, 14
Volatile principle, 8, 17, 20
Vriese, ix (*Pl. 17*)
Vulcan, 21

Washerwomen, 60
Water, 3, 5, 6, 8, 14, 59
Weiditz, viii, 23, 31, 33, 59, 62, 65, 68, 75, *Pl. 8*
Westminster Abbey, 56
Wetness, 60
Wheat, 14, 86
White Stone, 12
Wife, 63, 78, 81, 83
Wijck, ix, 78, 81, 83, 84, *Pls. 24, 25*
Wilton, 49
Wisdom of Solomon, 58
Wolf, 19
Woodcuts, 21, 22, 57
Wooden-legged man, 18, 19, 22, 60, 85
Wright, x, 86, 88, *Pl. 29*
Wyck. *See* Wijck

Zachaire, 28
Zlatá ulička, 11, 40
Zodiac, 14
Zoffany, ix, 41, *Pl. 12*
Zorg, 84

FINIS.